STAND OUT

Evidence-Based Learning for College and Career Readiness

BASIC

THIRD EDITION

ROB JENKINS

STACI JOHNSON

NATIONAL
GEOGRAPHIC
LEARNING

CENGAGE
Learning®

Australia • Brazil • Mexico • Singapore • United Kingdom • United States

**Stand Out Basic: Evidence-Based Learning
for College and Career Readiness,
Third Edition**
Rob Jenkins and Staci Johnson

Publisher: Sherrise Roehr

Executive Editor: Sarah Kenney

Development Editor: Lewis Thompson

Director of Global Marketing: Ian Martin

Executive Marketing Manager: Ben Rivera

Product Marketing Manager: Dalia Bravo

Director of Content and Media Production:
   Michael Burggren

Production Manager: Daisy Sosa

Media Researcher: Leila Hishmeh

Senior Print Buyer: Mary Beth Hennebury

Cover and Interior Designer:
   Brenda Carmichael

Composition: Lumina

Main Image: Portra Images/Getty Images

Bottom Images: (Left to Right) Jay B Sauceda/
   Getty Images; Tripod/Getty Images;
   Dear Blue/Getty Images; Portra Images/
   Getty Images; Mark Edward Atkinson/
   Tracey Lee/Getty Images; Hero Images/
   Getty Images; Jade/Getty Images; Seth Joel/
   Getty Images; LWA/Larry Williams/
   Getty Images; Dimitri Otis/Getty Images

For permission to use material from this text or product,
submit all requests online at **www.cengage.com/permissions**
Further permissions questions can be emailed to
permissionrequest@cengage.com

Student Book
ISBN 13: 978-1-305-65520-1

National Geographic Learning/Cengage Learning
20 Channel Center Street
Boston, MA 02210
USA

Cengage Learning is a leading provider of customized learning solutions with office locations around the globe, including Singapore, the United Kingdom, Australia, Mexico, Brazil, and Japan.

Cengage Learning products are represented in Canada by Nelson Education, Ltd.

Visit National Geographic Learning online at **ngl.cengage.com**
Visit our corporate website at **www.cengage.com**

Printed in the United States of America
Print Number: 09   Print Year: 2023

ACKNOWLEDGMENTS

Ellen Albano
Mcfatter Technical College, Davie, FL

Esther Anaya-Garcia
Glendale Community College, Glendale, AZ

Carol Bellamy
Prince George's Community College, Largo, MD

Gail Bier
Atlantic Technical College, Coconut Creek, FL

Kathryn Black
Myrtle Beach Family Learning Center, Myrtle Beach, SC

Claudia Brantley
College of Southern Nevada, Las Vegas, NV

Dr. Joan-Yvette Campbell
Lindsey Hopkins Technical College, Miami, FL

Maria Carmen Iglesias
Miami Senior Adult Educational Center, Miami, FL

Lee Chen
Palomar College, San Marcos, CA

Casey Cahill
Atlantic Technical College, Coconut Creek, FL

Maria Dillehay
Burien Job Training and Education Center, Goodwill, Seattle, WA

Irene Fjaerestad
Olympic College, Bremerton, WA

Eleanor Forfang-Brockman
Tarrant County College, Fort Worth, Texas

Jesse Galdamez
San Bernardino Adult School, San Bernardino, CA

Anna Garoz
Lindsey Hopkins Technical Education Center, Miami, FL

Maria Gutierrez
Miami Sunset Adult, Miami, FL

Noel Hernandez
Palm Beach County Public Schools, Palm Beach County, FL

Kathleen Hiscock
Portland Adult Education, Portland, ME

Frantz Jean-Louis
The English Center, Miami, FL

Annette Johnson
Sheridan Technical College, Hollywood, FL

Ginger Karaway
Gateway Technical College, Kenosha, WI

Judy Martin-Hall
Indian River State College, Fort Pierce, FL

Toni Molinaro
Dixie Hollins Adult Education Center, St Petersburg, FL

Tracey Person
Cape Cod Community College, Hyannis, MA

Celina Paula
Miami-Dade County Public Schools, Miami, FL

Veronica Pavon-Baker
Miami Beach Adult, Miami, FL

Ileana Perez
Robert Morgan Technical College, Miami, FL

Neeta Rancourt
Atlantic Technical College, Coconut Creek, FL

Brenda Roland
Joliet Junior College, Joliet, IL

Hidelisa Sampson
Las Vegas Urban League, Las Vegas, NV

Lisa Schick
James Madison University, Harrisonburg, VA

Rob Sheppard
Quincy Asian Resources, Quincy, MA

Sydney Silver
Burien Job Training and Education Center, Goodwill, Seattle, WA

Teresa Tamarit
Miami Senior Adult Educational Center, Miami, FL

Cristina Urena
Atlantic Technical College, Fort Lauderdale, FL

Pamela Jo Wilson
Palm Beach County Public Schools, Palm Beach County, FL

ABOUT THE AUTHORS

Rob Jenkins

I love teaching. I love to see the expressions on my students' faces when the light goes on and their eyes show such sincere joy of learning. I knew the first time I stepped into an ESL classroom that this is where I needed to be and I have never questioned that resolution. I have worked in business, sales, and publishing, and I've found challenge in all, but nothing can compare to the satisfaction of reaching people in such a personal way.

Staci Johnson

Ever since I can remember, I've been fascinated with other cultures and languages. I love to travel and every place I go, the first thing I want to do is meet the people, learn their language, and understand their culture. Becoming an ESL teacher was a perfect way to turn what I love to do into my profession. There's nothing more incredible than the exchange of teaching and learning from one another that goes on in an ESL classroom. And there's nothing more rewarding than helping a student succeed.

Along with the inclusion of National Geographic content, the third edition of **Stand Out** boasts of several innovations. In response to initiatives regarding the development of more complexity with reading and encouraging students to interact more with reading texts, we are proud to introduce new rich reading sections that allow students to discuss topics relevant to a global society. We have also introduced new National Geographic videos that complement the life-skill videos **Stand Out** introduced in the second edition and which are now integrated into the student books. We don't stop there; **Stand Out** has even more activities that require critical and creative thinking that serve to maximize learning and prepare students for the future. The third edition also has online workbooks. **Stand Out** was the first mainstream ESL textbook for adults to introduce a lesson plan format, hundreds of customizable worksheets, and project-based instruction. The third edition expands on these features in its mission to provide rich learning opportunities that can be exploited in different ways. We believe that with the innovative approach that made **Stand Out** a leader from its inception, the many new features, and the new look; programs, teachers, and students will find great success!

Stand Out Mission Statement:

Our goal is to give students challenging opportunities to be successful in their language learning experience so they develop confidence and become independent lifelong learners.

TO THE TEACHER

ABOUT THE SERIES

The **Stand Out** series is designed to facilitate *active* learning within life-skill settings that lead students to career and academic pathways. Each student book and its supplemental components in the six-level series expose students to competency areas most useful and essential for newcomers with careful treatment of level appropriate but challenging materials. Students grow academically by developing essential literacy and critical thinking skills that will help them find personal success in a changing and dynamic world.

THE STAND OUT PHILOSOPHY

Integrated Skills

In each of the five lessons of every unit, skills are introduced as they might be in real language use. They are in context and not separated into different sections of the unit. We believe that for real communication to occur, the classroom should mirror real-life as much as possible.

Objective Driven Activities

Every lesson in **Stand Out** is driven by a performance objective. These objectives have been carefully selected to ensure they are measurable, accessible to students at their particular level, and relevant to students and their lives. Good objectives lead to effective learning. Effective objectives also lead to appropriate self, student, and program assessment which is increasingly required by state and federal mandates.

Lesson Plan Sequencing

Stand Out follows an established sequence of activities that provides students with the tools they need to have in order to practice and apply the skills required in the objective. A pioneer in Adult Education for introducing the Madeline Hunter WIPPEA lesson plan model into textbooks, **Stand Out** continues to provide a clear and easy-to-follow system for presenting and developing English language skills. The WIPPEA model follows six steps:

* **W**arm up and Review
* **I**ntroduction
* **P**resentation
* **P**ractice
* **E**valuation
* **A**pplication

Learning And Acquisition

In **Stand Out**, the recycling of skills is emphasized. Students must learn and practice the same skills multiple times in various contexts to actually acquire them. Practicing a skill one time is rarely sufficient for acquisition and rarely addresses diverse student needs and learning styles.

Critical Thinking

Critical thinking has been defined in various ways and sometimes so broadly that any activity could be classified to meet the criteria. To be clear and to draw attention to the strong critical thinking activities in **Stand Out,** we define these activities as *tasks that require learners to think deeper than the superficial vocabulary and meaning.* Activities such as ranking, making predictions, analyzing, or solving problems, demand that students think beyond the surface. Critical thinking is highlighted throughout so the instructor can be confident that effective learning is going on.

Learner-Centered, Cooperative, and Communicative Activities

Stand Out provides ample opportunities for students to develop interpersonal skills and to practice new vocabulary through graphic organizers and charts like VENN diagrams, graphs, classifying charts, and mind maps. The lesson planners provide learner-centered approaches in every lesson. Students are asked to rank items, make decisions, and negotiate amongst other things.

Dialogues are used to prepare students for these activities in the low levels and fewer dialogues are used at the higher levels where students have already acquired the vocabulary and rudimentary conversation skills.

Activities should provide opportunities for students to speak in near authentic settings so they have confidence to perform outside the classroom. This does not mean that dialogues and other mechanical activities are not used to prepare students for cooperative activities, but these mechanical activities do not foster conversation. They merely provide the first tools students need to go beyond mimicry.

Assessment

Instructors and students should have a clear understanding of what is being taught and what is expected. In **Stand Out**, objectives are clearly stated so that target skills can be effectively assessed throughout.

Formative assessments are essential. Pre and post-assessments can be given for units or sections of the book through *ExamView*—a program that makes developing tests easy and effective. These tests can be created to appear like standardized tests, which are important for funding and to help students prepare.

Finally, *learner logs* allow students to self-assess, document progress, and identify areas that might require additional attention.

SUPPLEMENTAL COMPONENTS

The **Stand Out** series is a comprehensive one-stop for all student needs. There is no need to look any further than the resources offered.

Stand Out Lesson Planners

The lesson planners go beyond merely describing activities in the student book by providing teacher support, ideas, and guidance for the entire class period.

- **Standards correlations** for **CCRS, CASAS,** and **SCANS** are identified for each lesson.
- **Pacing Guides** help with planning by giving instructors suggested durations for each activity and a selection of activities for different class lengths.
- **Teacher Tips** provide point-of-use pedagogical comments and best practices.
- **At-A-Glance Lesson Openers** provide the instructor with everything that will be taught in a particular lesson. Elements include, the agenda, the goal, grammar, pronunciation, academic strategies, critical thinking elements, correlations to standards, and resources.
- **Suggested Activities** go beyond what is shown in the text providing teachers with ideas that will stimulate them to come up with their own.
- **Listening Scripts** are integrated into the unit pages for easy access.

Stand Out Workbook

The workbook in the third edition takes the popular **Stand Out Grammar Challenge** and expands it to include vocabulary building, life-skill development, and grammar practice associated directly with each lesson in the student book.

Stand Out Online Workbook

One of the most important innovations new to the third edition of **Stand Out** is the online workbook. This workbook provides unique activities that are closely related to the student book and gives students opportunities to have access to audio and video.

The online workbook provides opportunities for students to practice and improve digital literacy skills essential for 21st century learners. These skills are essential for standardized computer and online testing. Scores in these tests will improve when students can concentrate on the content and not so much on the technology.

Activity Bank

The Activity Bank is an online feature that provides several hundred multilevel worksheets per level to enhance the already rich materials available through **Stand Out**.

DVD Program

The **Stand Out Lifeskills Video Program** continues to be available with eight episodes per level; however, now the worksheets are part of the student books with additional help in the lesson planners.

New to the third edition of **Stand Out** are two National Geographic videos per level. Each video is accompanied by four pages of instruction and activities with support in the lesson planners.

Examview

ExamView is a program that provides customizable test banks and allows instructors to make lesson, unit, and program tests quickly.

STANDARDS AND CORRELATIONS

Stand Out is the pioneer in establishing a foundation of standards within each unit and through every objective. The standards movement in the United States is as dominant today as it was when **Stand Out** was first published. Schools and programs must be aware of on-going local and federal initiatives and make attempts to meet ever-changing requirements.

In the first edition of **Stand Out**, we identified direct correlations to SCANS, EFF, and CASAS standards. *The Secretaries Commission on Achieving Necessary Skills* or SCANS and *Equipped for the Future* or EFF standards are still important and are identified in every lesson of **Stand Out**. These skills include the basic skills, interpersonal skills, and problem-solving skills necessary to be successful in the workplace, in school, and in the community. **Stand Out** was also developed with a thorough understanding of objectives established by the *Comprehensive Adult Student Assessment Systems* or CASAS. Many programs have experienced great success with their CASAS scores using **Stand Out**, and these objectives continue to be reflected in the third edition.

Today, a new emphasis on critical thinking and complexity has swept the nation. Students are expected to think for themselves more now than ever before. They must also interact with reading texts at a higher level. These new standards and expectations are highly visible in the third edition and include *College and Career Readiness Standards.*

Stand Out offers a complete set of correlations online for all standards to demonstrate how closely we align with state and federal guidelines.

IMPORTANT INNOVATIONS TO THE THIRD EDITION

New Look
Although the third edition of **Stand Out** boasts of the same lesson plan format and task-based activities that made it one of the most popular books in adult education, it now has an updated look with the addition of the National Geographic content which will capture the attention of the instructor and every student.

Critical Thinking
With the advent of new federal and state initiatives, teachers need to be confident that students will use critical thinking skills when learning. This has always been a goal in **Stand Out**, but now those opportunities are highlighted in each lesson.

College And Career Readiness Skills
These skills are also identified by critical thinking strategies and academic-related activities which are found throughout **Stand Out**. New to the third edition is a special reading section in each unit that challenges students and encourages them to develop reading strategies within a rich National Geographic environment.

Stand Out Workbook
The print workbook is now more extensive and complete with vocabulary, life skills, and grammar activities to round out any program. Many instructors might find these pages ideal for homework, but they of course can be used for additional practice within the classroom.

Media And Online Support
Media and online support includes audio, video, online workbooks, presentation tools, and multi-level worksheets, ExamView, and standards correlations.

CONTENTS

Numeracy/ Academic Skills	CCRS	SCANS	CASAS
• Writing numerals 1-10 • Writing telephone numbers • Dictation • Focused listening • Class application • Test-taking skills	SL1, SL2, L2, RF2, RF3	**Many SCAN skills are incorporated in this unit with an emphasis on:** • Listening • Speaking • Writing • Sociability • Acquiring and evaluating information • Interpreting and communicating information	**1:** 0.1.1, 0.1.4, 0.2.1 **2:** 0.1.1, 0.1.4, 0.2.1 **3:** 0.1.5, 7.4.7
• Writing numerals 1-31 • Writing dates • Focused listening • Teamwork skills • Reviewing • Evaluating • Developing study skills	RI1, RI7, SL1, SL2, SL4, L1, L2, L5, RF2, RF3	**Many SCAN skills are incorporated in this unit with an emphasis on:** • Basic skills • Acquiring and evaluating information • Interpreting and communicating information • Seeing things in the mind's eye • Sociability	**1:** 0.1.1, 0.2.1 **2:** 0.1.2, 0.2.1, 1.1.3, 4.8.7 **3:** 0.1.2, 0.2.1 **4:** 0.1.2, 0.2.1, 1.1.3, 4.8.7 **5:** 0.1.2, 0.2.1, 2.3.2 **R:** 0.1.1, 0.2.1, 7.4.1, 7.4.2, 7.4.3 **TP:** 0.1.1, 0.2.1, 4.8.1
• Interpreting a bar graph • Telling time • Focused listening • Scheduling • Reviewing • Evaluating • Developing study skills	RI1, RI7, SL1, SL2, SL4, L1, L2, L4, L5, RF2, RF3	**Many SCAN skills are incorporated in this unit with an emphasis on:** • Acquiring and evaluating information • Organizing and maintaining information • Interpreting and communicating information • Basic skills • Reflect and Evaluate	**1:** 0.1.4 **2:** 0.1.5 **3:** 0.1.5 **4:** 0.2.1, 0.2.4, 2.3.1 **5:** 0.1.2, 0.2.1, 1.1.3, 2.3.3 **R:** 0.1.5, 2.3.1, 2.3.2, 2.3.3, 7.4.1, 7.4.2, 7.4.3 **TP:** 0.1.5, 2.3.1, 2.3.2, 2.3.3, 4.8.1

CONTENTS

Numeracy/Academic Skills	CCRS	SCANS	CASAS
• Using U.S. measurements: pounds, gallons • Working in a group • Focused listening • Skimming • Categorizing and organizing information • Teamwork skills • Reviewing • Evaluating • Developing study skills	RI1, RI7, RI9, W1, W2, SL1, SL2, SL4, L1, L2, L5, RF2, RF3	**Many SCAN skills are incorporated in this unit with an emphasis on:** • Acquiring and evaluating information • Organizing and maintaining information • Interpreting and communicating information • Allocating human resources • Basic skills • Seeing things in the mind's eye	**1:** 1.3.8 **2:** 1.3.8 **3:** 1.1.1, 1.3.8 **4:** 1.3.8 **5:** 1.3.8 **R:** 1.3.8, 7.4.1, 7.4.2, 7.4.3 **TP:** 1.8.8, 4.8.1
• Using U.S. measurements: clothing sizes • Maintaining inventories • Counting U.S. money • Calculating totals • Writing checks • Asking for information • Focused listening • Test-taking skills • Reviewing • Evaluating • Developing study skills	RI1, RI7, SL1, SL2, SL4, L1, L2, L3, L5, RF2, RF3	**Many SCAN skills are incorporated in this unit with an emphasis on:** • Acquiring and evaluating information • Organizing and maintaining information • Interpreting and communicating information • Basic skills • Allocating money • Serving clients and customers	**1:** 1.2.1, 1.3.9 **2:** 1.3.9 **3:** 1.1.9, 1.2.1, 1.3.9 **4:** 1.1.6, 1.3.9, 4.8.1, 6.1.1 **5:** 1.1.9, 1.2.1, 1.3.9, 4.8.3 **R:** 1.1.9, 1.2.1, 1.3.9, 7.4.1, 7.4.2, 7.4.3 **TP:** 1.3.9, 4.8.1
• Interpreting a bar graph • Creating a bar graph • Test-taking strategies • Focused listening • Dictation • Reviewing • Evaluating • Developing study skills	RI1, RI7, SL1, SL2, SL3, SL4, L1, L2, L3, L5, RF2, RF3	**Many SCAN skills are incorporated in this unit with an emphasis on:** • Acquiring and evaluating information • Organizing and maintaining information • Interpreting and communicating information • Basic skills • Creative thinking • Participating as a member of a team	**1:** 1.3.7, 7.2.3 **2:** 1.4.1, 1.4.2, 1.9.4 **3:** 1.1.3, 2.2.3, 2.2.5, 6.7.2 **4:** 0.1.2, 0.2.4 **5:** 1.1.3, 1.9.1, 1.9.4, 2.2.1, 2.2.2, 2.5.4 **R:** 2.2.3, 7.4.1, 7.4.2, 7.4.3 **TP:** 2.2.3, 4.8.1

CONTENTS

Numeracy/Academic Skills	CCRS	SCANS	CASAS
• Focused listening • Test-taking skills • Reviewing • Evaluating • Developing study skills	RI1, RI2, RI7, W1, W2, SL1, SL2, SL4, L1, L2, L3, L5, RF2, RF3	**Many SCAN skills are incorporated in this unit with an emphasis on:** • Acquiring and evaluating information • Organizing and maintaining information • Interpreting and communicating information • Basic skills • Self-management • Responsibility	**1:** 3.1.1, 3.1.3 **2:** 0.1.2, 0.2.1, 3.1.1 **3:** 2.3.1, 3.1.2, 3.3.1 **4:** 3.1.1 **5:** 3.1.3 **R:** 3.1.1, 3.1.2, 3.1.3, 3.3.1 **TP:** 1.3.9, 4.8.1
• Focused listening • Making graphs • Reviewing • Evaluating • Developing study skills	RI1, RI7, W2, SL1, SL2, L1, L2, L5, RF2, RF3	**Many SCAN skills are incorporated in this unit with an emphasis on:** • Acquiring and evaluating information • Organizing and maintaining information • Interpreting and communicating information • Basic skills • Self-management	**1:** 0.2.1, 4.1.8 **2:** 0.1.6, 4.8.1 **3:** 4.1.3, 4.1.8, 4.4.4 **4:** 4.4.4 **5:** 4.4.4, 4.8.1, 4.8.3 **R:** 4.1.3, 4.1.8, 4.4.1, 4.8.1, 4.8.3, 7.4.1, 7.4.2, 7.4.3 **TP:** 2.2.3, 4.8.1
• Identifying quantities and sizes • Calculating totals • Reading telephone numbers • Interpreting a bar graph • Focused listening • Test-taking skills • Organizational skills • Reviewing • Evaluating • Developing study skills	RI1, RI2, RI7, W2, SL1, SL2, SL4, L1, L2, L5, RF2, RF3	**Many SCAN skills are incorporated in this unit with an emphasis on:** • Acquiring and evaluating information • Organizing and maintaining information • Interpreting and communicating information • Basic skills • Self-management	**1:** 0.2.1, 0.2.2, 7.1.4 **2:** 1.1.6, 1.2.1, 1.3.1, 1.6.4, 7.1.4 **3:** 2.1.1, 2.2.1, 7.1.4 **4:** 0.2.1, 3.5.9, 6.7.2, 7.1.1, 7.1.2, 7.1.4 **5:** 4.1.1, 4.4.4, 7.1.1, 7.1.4 **R:** 7.4.2, 7.4.3 **TP:** 2.2.3, 4.8.1

Appendices

For other national and state specific standards, please visit: **www.NGL.Cengage.com/SO3**

INTRODUCING
STAND OUT, Third Edition!

Stand Out is a six-level, standards-based ESL series for adult education with a proven track record of successful results. The new edition of *Stand Out* continues to provide students with the foundations and tools needed to achieve success in life, college, and career.

Stand Out now integrates real-world content from National Geographic

UNIT 1

Balancing Your Life

UNIT OUTCOMES
- Analyze and create schedules
- Identify goals and obstacles and suggest solutions
- Write about a personal goal
- Analyze study habits
- Manage time

Look at the photo and answer the questions.
1. What do you think the people are doing?
2. What activities do you do every day?
3. What do you want to do in the future?

Construction workers on beams at the top of the Stratosphere Tower in Las Vegas.

- Stand Out now integrates high-interest, real-world content from National Geographic which enhances its proven approach to lesson planning and instruction. A stunning National Geographic image at the beginning of each unit introduces the theme and engages learners in meaningful conversations right from the start.

Stand Out supports college and career readiness

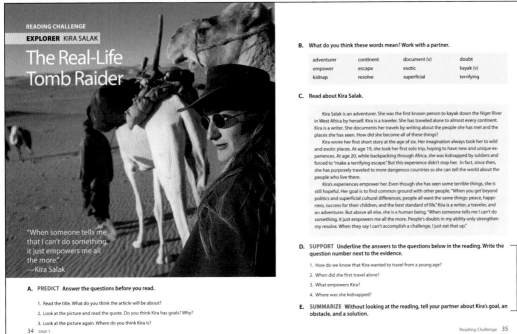

- Carefully crafted activities help prepare students for college and career success.

- **NEW Reading Challenge** in every unit features a fascinating story about a **National Geographic explorer** to immerse learners in authentic content.

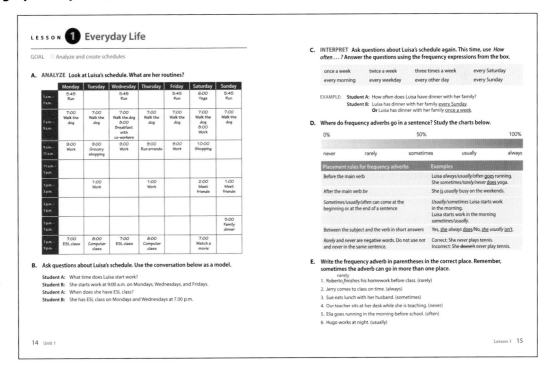

- **EXPANDED Critical Thinking Activities** challenge learners to evaluate, analyze, and synthesize information to prepare them for the workplace and academic life.

- **NEW Video Challenge** showcases **National Geographic footage and explorers**, providing learners with the opportunity to synthesize what they have learned in prior units through the use of authentic content.

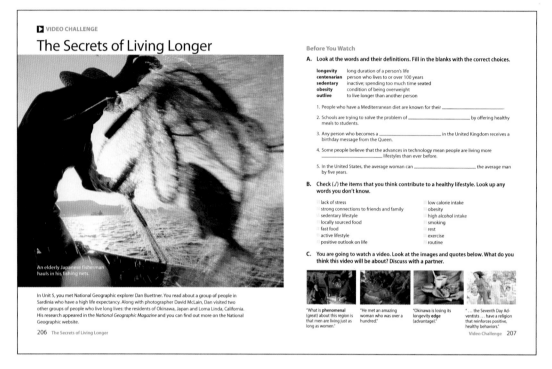

▶ VIDEO CHALLENGE

The Secrets of Living Longer

An elderly Japanese fisherman hauls in his fishing nets.

In Unit 5, you met National Geographic explorer Dan Buettner. You read about a group of people in Sardinia who have a high life expectancy. Along with photographer David McLain, Dan visited two other groups of people who live long lives: the residents of Okinawa, Japan and Loma Linda, California. His research appeared in the *National Geographic Magazine* and you can find out more on the National Geographic website.

206 The Secrets of Living Longer

Before You Watch

A. Look at the words and their definitions. Fill in the blanks with the correct choices.

longevity	long duration of a person's life
centenarian	person who lives to or over 100 years
sedentary	inactive; spending too much time seated
obesity	condition of being overweight
outlive	to live longer than another person

1. People who have a Mediterranean diet are known for their _____

2. Schools are trying to solve the problem of _____ by offering healthy meals to students.

3. Any person who becomes a _____ in the United Kingdom receives a birthday message from the Queen.

4. Some people believe that the advances in technology mean people are living more _____ lifestyles than ever before.

5. In the United States, the average woman can _____ the average man by five years.

B. Check (✓) the items that you think contribute to a healthy lifestyle. Look up any words you don't know.

☐ lack of stress	☐ low calorie intake
☐ strong connections to friends and family	☐ obesity
☐ sedentary lifestyle	☐ high alcohol intake
☐ locally sourced food	☐ smoking
☐ fast food	☐ rest
☐ active lifestyle	☐ exercise
☐ positive outlook on life	☐ routine

C. You are going to watch a video. Look at the images and quotes below. What do you think this video will be about? Discuss with a partner.

"What is **phenomenal** (great) about this region is that men are living just as long as women."

"He met an amazing woman who was over a hundred."

"Okinawa is losing its longevity **edge** (advantage)."

" ... the Seventh Day Adventists ... have a religion that reinforces positive, healthy behaviors."

Video Challenge 207

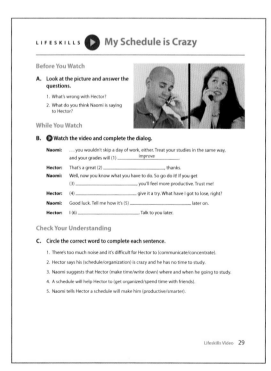

LIFESKILLS ▶ **My Schedule is Crazy**

Before You Watch

A. Look at the picture and answer the questions.

1. What's wrong with Hector?

2. What do you think Naomi is saying to Hector?

While You Watch

B. ▶ Watch the video and complete the dialog.

Naomi: ... you wouldn't skip a day of work, either. Treat your studies in the same way, and your grades will (1) _____improve_____

Hector: That's a great (2) _____, thanks.

Naomi: Well, now you know what you have to do. So go do it! If you get (3) _____, you'll feel more productive. Trust me!

Hector: (4) _____ give it a try. What have I got to lose, right?

Naomi: Good luck. Tell me how it's (5) _____ later on.

Hector: I (6) _____ Talk to you later.

Check Your Understanding

C. Circle the correct word to complete each sentence.

1. There's too much noise and it's difficult for Hector to (communicate/concentrate).

2. Hector says his (schedule/organization) is crazy and he has no time to study.

3. Naomi suggests that Hector (make time/write down) where and when he going to study.

4. A schedule will help Hector to (get organized/spend time with friends).

5. Naomi tells Hector a schedule will make him (productive/smarter).

Lifeskills Video 29

- The **Lifeskills Video** is a dramatic video series integrated into each unit of the student book that helps students learn natural spoken English and apply it to their everyday activities.

Pages shown are from *Stand Out*, Third Edition Level 3

- **NEW Online Workbook** engages students and supports the classroom by providing a wide variety of auto-graded interactive activities, an audio program, video from National Geographic, and pronunciation activities.

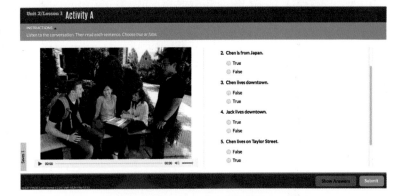

- **UPDATED Lesson Planner** includes correlations to **College and Career Readiness Standards (CCRS)**, **CASAS, SCANS** and reference to **EL Civics** competencies to help instructors achieve the required standards.

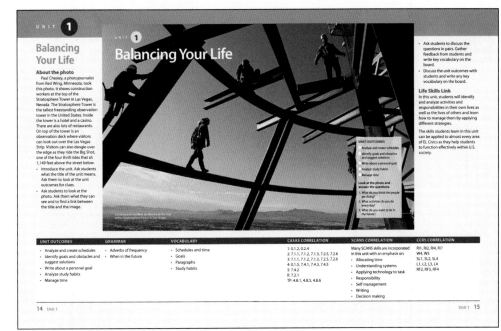

- **Teacher support** Stand Out continues to provide a wide variety of user-friendly tools and interactive activities that help teachers prepare students for success while keeping them engaged and motivated.

Stand Out supports teachers and learners

LEARNER COMPONENTS

- Student Book
- Online workbook powered by My**ELT**
- Print workbook

TEACHER COMPONENTS

- Lesson Planner
- Classroom DVD
- Assessment CD-ROM
- Teacher's companion site with Multi-Level Worksheets

Welcome

UNIT OUTCOMES

- Greet people
- Say and write phone numbers
- Follow instructions

LESSON ❶ Say hello!

GOAL ▪ Greet people

🎧 **A. Listen.**
CD 1
TR 1-2

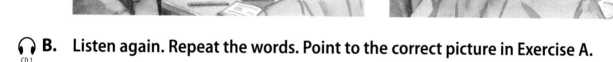

| hello | hi | goodbye | bye |

🎧 **B. Listen again. Repeat the words. Point to the correct picture in Exercise A.**
CD 1
TR 1-2

Greeting your friend is different from greeting your teacher.

C. Listen and point to the pictures. Who is speaking?
CD 1
TR 3-4

Orlando

Ms. Adams

Amal

Hang

D. Listen and repeat.
CD 1
TR 5

/m/
I'm Orlando.
I'm Ms. Adams.
I'm Amal.
I'm Hang.
I'm a student.

CONTRACTIONS
I am = *I'm*

E. Listen again and read.
CD 1
TR 3-4

Ms. Adams:	Hello. I'm Ms. Adams.
Orlando:	Hi, Ms. Adams. I'm Orlando. Nice to meet you.
Ms. Adams:	Nice to meet you, too.
Orlando:	Bye.
Ms. Adams:	Goodbye.
Hang:	Hi. I'm Hang.
Amal:	Hello, Hang. I'm Amal.
Hang:	Nice to meet you.
Amal:	Nice to meet you, too.
Hang:	Bye now.
Amal:	Bye.

F. Listen and repeat. Write the alphabet and your name.

CD 1
TR 6

Aa Bb Cc Dd Ee Ff Gg Hh Ii

Jj Kk Ll Mm Nn Oo Pp Qq Rr

Ss Tt Uu Vv Ww Xx Yy Zz

I'm Amal.

G. Write.

Hi

Hello

Goodbye

H. Write your name and a classmate's name. Then, talk to four more classmates.

Hi. I'm _____. (your name)

Hello. I'm _____. (classmate's name)

LESSON ② Phone numbers

GOAL ▮ Say and write phone numbers

🎧 **A.** **Listen and point. Who is speaking?**
CD 1
TR 7

🎧 **B.** **Listen and repeat. Point to each number. Then, write all the numbers.**
CD 1
TR 8

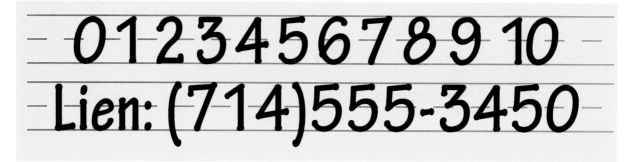

0 1 2 3 4 5 6 7 8 9 10
Lien: (714)555-3450

C. Listen and circle.

CD 1
TR 9

1.

Mai

(714) 555-7682
(714) 555-3450
(714) 555-7689

2.

Paulo

(352) 555-6767
(352) 555-1415
(352) 555-2655

3.

Ms. Banks

(808) 555-4512
(808) 555-6755
(808) 555-3456

4.

Ali

(915) 555-4576
(915) 555-3466
(915) 555-3455

D. Write.

1. Mai's phone number is ___(714) 555-3450_____.

2. Paulo's phone number is _____.

3. Ms. Banks' phone number is _____.

4. Ali's phone number is _____.

E. Listen and write the numbers.

CD 1
TR 10

1. _____

2. _____

3. _____

4. _____

5. _____

6. _____

F. Read the phone list.

PHONE LIST Ms. Adams' English Class	
Name	**Phone Number**
Hang	(714) 555-3450
Andre	(714) 555-1333
Shiro	(714) 555-9812
Sara	(714) 555-4545
Taylor	(714) 555-1237

G. Ask your partner for the phone numbers from Exercise F and write.

Student A: Hang
Student B: (714) 555-3450

The Verb *Be*
I *am* …
The phone number *is* …

Student A

Andre (_____) _____

Shiro (_____) _____

Student B

Sara   (_____) _____

Taylor (_____) _____

H. Make a class phone list.

PHONE LIST	
Name	**Phone number**
(my name)	

GOAL ▧ Follow instructions

🎧 **A. Listen.**

CD 1
TR 11

🎧 **B. Listen again and point.**

CD 1
TR 11

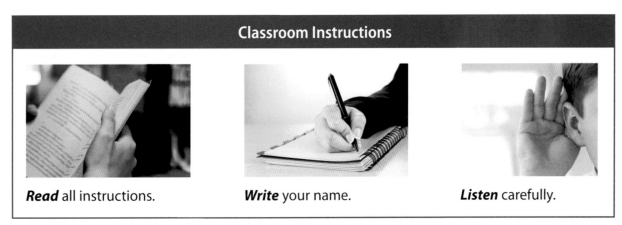

Classroom Instructions		
Read all instructions.	**Write** your name.	**Listen** carefully.

C. Write the actions.

repeat	read	listen	write	point

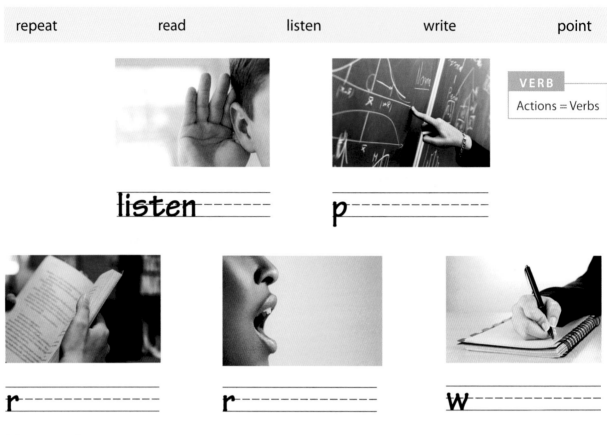

VERB

Actions = Verbs

listen - - - - - - - - - -

p - - - - - - - - - - -

r - - - - - - - - - - -

r - - - - - - - - - - -

w - - - - - - - - - - -

CD 1
TR 12

D. Listen and repeat.

/t/

Write.

Point.

Repeat.

E. Practice the actions in Exercise C.

EXAMPLE

Student A: Listen.

Student B:

F. Read and complete.

Circle.

1. pencil

  a. pen   b. (pencil)   c. paper

2. paper

  a. paper   b. pen   c. pencil

Check (✓).

3. pencil

  ☐ pen   ☐ pencil   ☐ paper

4. pen

  ☐ pen   ☐ paper   ☐ pencil

CD 1 TR 13

G. Listen and circle the answers.

1. a. point   b. repeat   c. listen   d. read   e. write

2. a. point   b. repeat   c. listen   d. read   e. write

3. a. point   b. repeat   c. listen   d. read   e. write

4. a. point   b. repeat   c. listen   d. read   e. write

CD 1 TR 14

H. Listen and check (✓) the answers.

1. ☐ a. point   ☐ b. repeat   ☐ c. listen   ☐ d. read   ☐ e. write

2. ☐ a. point   ☐ b. repeat   ☐ c. listen   ☐ d. read   ☐ e. write

3. ☐ a. point   ☐ b. repeat   ☐ c. listen   ☐ d. read   ☐ e. write

4. ☐ a. point   ☐ b. repeat   ☐ c. listen   ☐ d. read   ☐ e. write

I. Follow the instructions.

1. Circle the phone number.

  02219   (212) 555-7763   04/08/09   7.1.2015

2. Check (✓) the answer.

  $2 + 2 =$ _____   ☐ 3   ☐ 5   ☐ 4

3. Write the name of your teacher.

_____

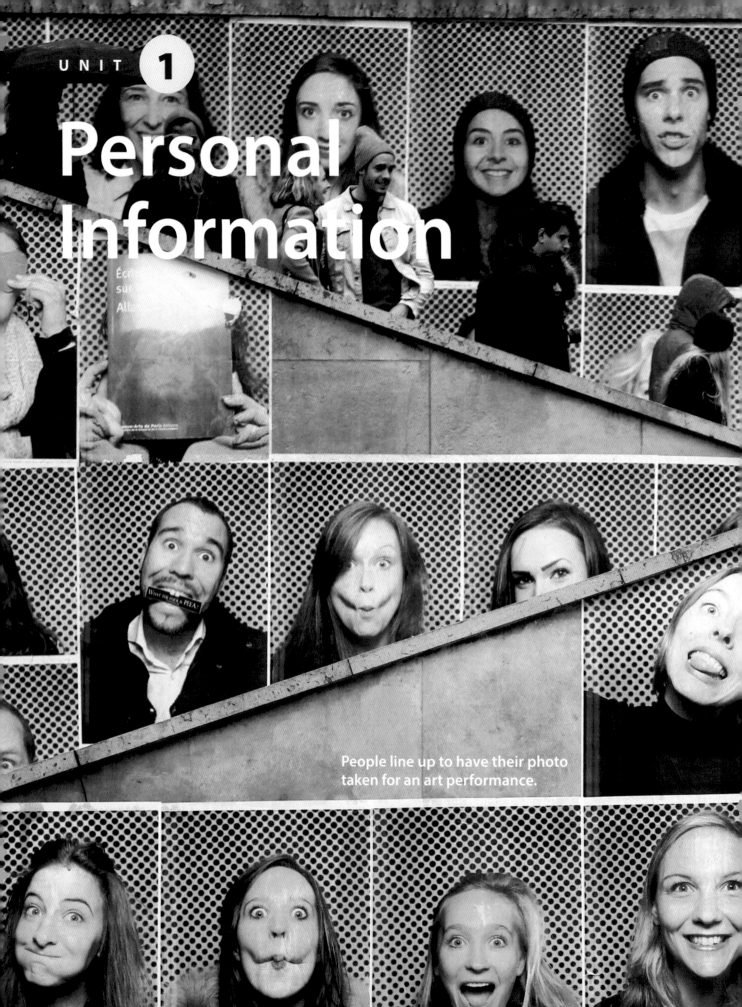

Personal Information

People line up to have their photo taken for an art performance.

UNIT OUTCOMES

- ☐ Identify people
- ☐ Express nationalities
- ☐ Express marital status
- ☐ Say and write addresses
- ☐ Say and write dates

Look at the photo and answer the questions.

1. Where are the people in the pictures from?
2. How old are they?

GOAL ▓ Identify people

🎧 **A. IDENTIFY** Listen and point.
CD 1
TR 15

What's his name?
His name is Amal.

What's her name?
Her name is Ms. Adams.

What are their names?
Their names are Hang and Elsa.

What's your name?
My name is ...

B. Practice the conversation. Use the questions in Exercise A to make new conversations.

Student A: What's his name?
Student B: His name is Amal.

INTONATION

What's your name?

C. Listen and repeat.

CD 1
TR 16

I

You

He

She

We

They

D. RELATE Look again at the pictures in Exercise A. Write.

1. His name is Amal. _____He_____ is a student.

2. Her name is Ms. Adams. _____ is a teacher.

3. Their names are Hang and Elsa. _____ are students.

4. My name is _____. _____ am a student.

E. Listen and point.

CD 1
TR 17

Hang:	Hi, Satsuki.
Satsuki:	Hello, Hang.
Hang:	Elsa, this is Satsuki. He is a student.
Elsa:	Hello, Satsuki. I am a student, too.
Satsuki:	Nice to meet you.

> **THIS IS …**
> We use *This is …*
> to introduce people.

F. Practice the conversation in Exercise E.

G. CLASSIFY Work with a partner. Write classmates' names.

Pronoun		Name
I	I am a student.	(your name)
You	You are a student.	(your partner's name)
He	He is a student.	
She	She is a student.	
We	We are students.	
They	They are students.	

GOAL   Express nationalities

A. Read and listen.

CD 1
TR 18

B. Write.

1. What's her name? _____

2. Where is she from? _____

C. Ask your classmates.

1. What's your name?

2. Where are you from?

D. SURVEY Ask about other classmates.

1. What's his name? What's her name?

2. Where's he from? Where's she from?

E. PREDICT Look at the picture and answer the questions.

1. Where is Shiro from? _____

2. Where is Amal from? _____

3. Where is Hang from? _____

4. Where is Elsa from? _____

🎧 **F. Listen and write.**

CD 1
TR 19-23

1. She is from Cuba. _____ *Sara* _____

2. He is from Lebanon. _____

3. She is from Vietnam. _____

4. She is from Russia. _____

5. He is from Japan. _____

G. Practice the conversations. Use the information in Exercise F to make new conversations.

Student A: Where is <u>Sara</u> from?   **Student A:** What's her birthplace?
Student B: She is from <u>Cuba</u>.   **Student B:** <u>Cuba</u>.

BIRTHPLACE
Where is he from? He is from Japan.
What's his birthplace? Japan.

H. Read.

Simple Present		
I	live	in Los Angeles.
He	lives	in Irvine.
She		in Chicago.

I. Complete the sentences.

1. Sara _is from Cuba_____. She _lives_____ in Irvine.

2. Shiro _____. He _____ in Irvine.

3. Amal _____. He _____ in Irvine.

4. Elsa _____. She _____ in Irvine.

5. Hang _____. She _____ in Irvine.

6. I am from _____. I _____.

J. Practice the conversation. Use the information in Exercise I to make new conversations.

CD 1
TR 24

Ms. Adams: Hi, <u>Sara</u>. Where are you from?
Sara: I'm from <u>Cuba</u>.
Ms. Adams: Where do you live?
Sara: I live in <u>Irvine</u>.

K. APPLY Ask four classmates. Make new conversations and complete the table.

You: Hi, _____. Where are you from?

Classmate: I'm from _____.

You: Where do you live?

Classmate: I live in _____.

Name (What's your name?)	Birthplace (Where are you from?)	Current city (Where do you live?)
1.		
2.		
3.		
4.		

LESSON ❸ Are you married?

GOAL ▮ Express marital status

CD 1
TR 25

A. IDENTIFY Listen and write.

single	married	divorced

He is _____.

They are _____.   They are _____.

B. With a partner, point at the pictures in Exercise A and say: *He is single, They are married*, or *They are divorced*.

C. Read.

The Verb *Be*			
Pronoun	**Be**	**Marital status**	**Example sentence**
I	am	married	I am married.
He	is	single	He is single. (Amed is single.)
She		divorced	She is divorced. (Mirna is divorced.)
We		divorced	We are divorced.
You	are	married	You are married.
They		single	They are single.

D. PREDICT Are they married, single, or divorced? Circle *yes* or *no*. Then, listen and write.

CD 1
TR 26

1.

Maria

Is she married?   Yes   No

She _____.

2.

Hans

Is he married?   Yes   No

He _____.

3.

Mr. and Mrs. Johnson

Are they married?   Yes   No

They _____.

E. Write *am*, *is*, or *are*.

1. Mr. and Mrs. Johnson _____*are*_____ married.

2. Orlando _____ divorced.

3. Omar, Natalie, and Doug _____ single.

4. We _____ divorced.

5. They _____ single.

6. She _____ married.

7. We _____ single.

8. You _____ married.

F. Read and write the contractions.

1. I + am = I'm	_____ I'm _____ married.
2. You + are = You're	_____ divorced.
3. He + is = He's	_____ single.
4. She + is = She's	_____ divorced.
5. We + are = We're	_____ married.
6. They + are = They're	_____ single.

G. Complete the sentences with the verbs. Rewrite each sentence with a contraction.

1. We _____ are _____ married.   We're married. _____

2. They _____ divorced.   _____

3. I _____ single.   _____

4. He _____ divorced.   _____

5. You _____ married.   _____

6. She _____ single.   _____

H. Read.

A: Hans, are you married?	**A:** Lin, are you married?	**A:** Pam, are you married?
B: No, I'm single.	**B:** Yes, I'm married.	**B:** No, I'm divorced.

I. CLASSIFY Speak to five classmates.

Name	Marital status (Are you married?)
Hans	single
1.	
2.	
3.	
4.	
5.	

GOAL Say and write addresses

A. Read.

IRVINE PUBLIC LIBRARY

FIRST NAME: **Safa**
LAST NAME: **Ahadi**
STREET ADDRESS: **2687 Westpark Lane**
CITY: **Irvine**
STATE: **CA**
ZIP: **92714**

B. Write.

First name: _Safa_

Last name: _Ahadi_

Street address: _____

City: _____

State: _____

Zip code: _____

C. IDENTIFY Listen and point to the addresses.

CD 1
TR 27

3259 Lincoln Street   51 Apple Avenue   12367 Elm Road

The President of the United States lives at 1600 Pennsylvania Avenue, Washington, DC 20500.

D. Listen to the addresses. Write the numbers only.

1. _____ 2. _____ 3. _____ 4. _____

E. Listen and write.

COMMAS
Use commas (,) to separate the different parts of an address.

LOCKE ADULT SCHOOL

FIRST NAME:	**Amal**
LAST NAME:	**Jahshan**
STREET ADDRESS:	**8237 Augustin Street**
CITY:	**Irvine**
STATE:	**CA**
ZIP:	**92602**

Amal Jahshan

8883242442v

Address:

_____8237_____ Augustin Street,

Irvine, CA 92602

IRVINE PUBLIC LIBRARY

FIRST NAME:	**Hang**
LAST NAME:	**Tran**
STREET ADDRESS:	_____ **Fin Road**
CITY:	**Irvine**
STATE:	**CA**
ZIP:	**92602**

x Hang Tran

Address:

_____ Fin Road,

Irvine, CA 92602

CUSTOMER SERVICES

FIRST NAME:	**Elsa**
LAST NAME:	**Kusmin**
STREET ADDRESS:	_____ **San Andrew Street**
CITY:	**Irvine**
STATE:	**CA**
ZIP:	**92602**

Elsa Kusmin

Address:

_____ San Andrew Street,

Irvine, CA 92602

F. RELATE Write the addresses.

Name	Address
Amal	8237 Augustin Street, Irvine, CA 92602
Hang	
Elsa	

Hang: Hi, Amal. What's your address?
Amal: Hello, Hang. My address is 8237 Augustin Street, Irvine, California 92602.
Hang: Thanks.

The Verb *Be*		
Subject	**Be**	**Example Sentence**
He	is	He is a student.
She		She is a student.
It (address)		My address is 8237 Augustin Street, Irvine, California 92602.

H. Practice the conversations. Student A look at this page. Student B look at your answers in Exercise F. Write.

Student A: Hi, Amal. What's your address?
Student B: Hello, Elsa. My address is 8237 Augustin Street, _____.
Student A: Thanks.

Student A: Hi, Elsa. What's your address?
Student B: Hello, Amal. My address is _____.
Student A: Thanks.

Student A: Hi, Hang. What's your address?
Student B: Hello, Amal. My address is _____.
Student A: Thanks.

I. APPLY Ask your partner and write the information. Then ask two more classmates.

Name	Address

LESSON ⑤ What's your date of birth?

A. **Write this year.** _____

B. **LABEL** Write the month and the year. Circle today's date.

		1	2	3	4	5
6	7	8	9	10	11	12
13	14	15	16	17	18	19
20	21	22	23	24	25	26
27	28	29	30	31		

C. **Number the months.**

January	February	March	April
01	_____	_____	_____

May	June	July	August
_____	_____	_____	_____

September	October	November	December
09	_____	_____	_____

D. **Listen to the months and say the number. Listen again and write the months on a sheet of paper.**

CD 1
TR 31

December 5th, 1990: Norman Vaughn's 89th birthday, celebrated on Mount Vaughn.

E. Read.

Month	Day	Year	
September	21	2016	September 21st, 2016 09/21/2016
December	5	1990	December 5th, 1990 12/05/1990
August	2	1974	August 2nd, 1974 08/2/1974

ORDINAL NUMBERS

Notice how to write and say dates with words and numbers.

1st, 2nd, 3rd, 4th, 5th, 6th, 7th, 8th, 9th, 10th

January 1st	January 20th
January 2nd	January 21st
January 3rd	January 22nd
January 4th	January 30th
January 5th	January 31st

F. IDENTIFY Write the dates with words and numbers (December 5th, 1990).

1. The date today: _____

2. Your date of birth: _____

3. The date tomorrow: _____

4. Your friend's date of birth: _____

G. IDENTIFY Write the dates with numbers only (12/05/1990).

1. The date today: _____

2. Your date of birth: _____

3. The date tomorrow: _____

4. Your friend's date of birth: _____

CD 1
TR 32

H. Listen and write the dates.

Today	Date of birth
1.	
2.	
3.	

I. APPLY Practice the conversation. Use the information in Exercise H to make new conversations.

Student A: What's the date today?
Student B: It's June 25th.
Student A: Thanks.
Student A: What's your date of birth?
Student B: It's July 3rd, 1988.
Student A: Thanks.

> **CONTRACTIONS**
> What is = *What's*
> It is = *It's*

J. Develop a list of important class dates. Ask your teacher for help.

1. Today's date: _____

2. First day of school: _____

3. Holidays: _____

_____

_____

4. Last day of school: _____

July 4: Independence Day in the United States.

LIFESKILLS  Nice to meet you

Before You Watch

A. **Look at the picture and answer the questions.**

1. Where are the people?

2. Who is the person standing at the front?

While You Watch

B. **▶ Watch the video and circle the names you hear.**

Roger

Frank

Mateo

Edgar

Mrs. Smith

James

Hector

Linda

Naomi

Check Your Understanding

C. **Read the statements. Write *T* for true and *F* for false.**

1. Mrs. Smith is from California. ___F___

2. Hector lives in Boston. _____

3. Mateo is from Puerto Rico. _____

4. Naomi is from Pasadena. _____

5. Naomi works in a diner. _____

A. Read.

Yolanda Alvarez

First Name:	Yolanda
Last Name:	Alvarez
Date of Birth:	August 12th, 1977
Birthplace:	Mexico
Address:	2347 Oxford Drive
City:	Anaheim
State:	CA
Zip:	92807

B. Write.

1. What's her first name?

_____

2. What's her last name?

_____

3. What's her address?

_____

4. What's her date of birth?

_____

5. What's her birthplace?

_____

C. Speak to a partner. Write.

What's your first name?   What's your last name?

What's your address?   What's your phone number?

D. Write.

single	married	divorced
_____	_____	_____

Learner Log

I can identify people. I can express nationalities.
☐ Yes ☐ No ☐ Maybe   ☐ Yes ☐ No ☐ Maybe

E. Circle.

1.

She / He / They is from Germany.

2.

She / He / They is Ron Carter.

3.

She / He / They are in school.

4.

She / He / We live in Irvine.

F. Write the correct form of the verb *Be*. Then, write each sentence with a contraction.

1. She _____is_____ a student. _____She's a student._____

2. She _____ from Japan. _____

3. We _____ students at The Adult School. _____

4. They _____ from Honduras. _____

5. I _____ in school. _____

G. Write *live* or *lives*.

1. He _____ in Portugal.

2. I _____ in Chicago.

3. She _____ in the United States.

TEAM PROJECT ✓ Make a class book

COLLABORATE Form a team with four or five students. In your team, you need:

Position	Job description	Student name
Student 1: Team Leader	Check that everyone speaks English. Check that everyone participates.	
Student 2: Writer	Write information.	
Student 3: Artist	Draw pictures.	
Students 4/5: Spokespeople	Organize presentation.	

1. Make a table like the one below.

2. Write the information for the members of your team.

What's your first name?	
What's your last name?	
What's your address?	
What's your phone number?	
What's your date of birth?	
What's your marital status?	

3. Draw a picture or add a photo of each member.

4. Make a team book.

5. Do a presentation about your team.

6. Make a class book with the other teams.

Jimmy Chin
Read more about Jimmy in Unit 5.

Sarah Marquis
Read more about Sarah in Unit 4.

Diana Nyad
Read more about Diana in Unit 6.

Maritza Morales Casanova
Read more about Maritza in Unit 8.

A. PREDICT Look at the pictures. Answer the questions.

1. Who lives in Mexico? _____

2. Who was born in 1973? _____

3. Who lives in Switzerland? _____

4. Who is from New York City? _____

B. PREDICT Look at the pictures again. Put a check (✓) in the table.

	Adventurer	Teacher	Swimmer	Climber
Sarah Marquis				
Jimmy Chin				
Diana Nyad				
Maritza Morales Casanova				

C. Read about the explorers.

Sarah Marquis

Sarah Marquis is from Switzerland. She is an adventurer and a National Geographic explorer. Her date of birth is June 20th, 1972.

Jimmy Chin

Jimmy Chin is from Mankato, Minnesota. He is a climber and photographer. He is also a National Geographic explorer. He was born in 1973.

Diana Nyad

Diana Nyad is from New York City. Her birth date is August 22nd, 1949. She is a swimmer and a National Geographic explorer.

Maritza Morales Casanova

Maritza Morales Casanova is a teacher and a National Geographic explorer. She is from Mexico. She was born in 1985.

D. IDENTIFY Underline the date of birth in each paragraph.

E. CREATE Complete the sentences about the explorers.

1. Sarah Marquis is an _____.

2. Jimmy Chin is from _____.

3. Diana Nyad is from _____.

4. Maritza Morales Casanova is a _____.

UNIT **2**

Our Class

University students practice on models in a dentistry class.

UNIT OUTCOMES

◼ Introduce yourself and others

◼ Describe your surroundings

◼ Identify common activities

◼ Plan a schedule

◼ Plan for weather

Look at the photo and answer the questions.

1. What can you see in the classroom?

2. What are the students doing?

LESSON **1** Meet my friend

GOAL ▉ Introduce yourself and others

A. PREDICT Look at the picture. Where are the students from?

🎧 B. Listen and practice.

CD 1
TR 33

   I want to introduce two new students today. This is Edgar. He is from Senegal. He lives in Sacramento. His phone number is (916) 555-3765.

   Meet Julie. She is also a new student. She is from Canada. She lives in Folsom. Her number is (916) 555-4565.

C. CLASSIFY Write the information about Edgar and Julie.

Name	Phone	City
Edgar		
Julie		

D. Read the chart.

Possessive Adjectives		
Subject	**Possessive adjective**	**Example sentence**
I	My	**My** phone number is 555-3456.
You	Your	**Your** address is 2359 Maple Drive.
He	His	**His** name is Edgar.
She	Her	**Her** name is Julie.
We	Our	**Our** last name is Perez.
They	Their	**Their** teacher is Mr. Jackson.

E. RELATE Look at the pictures and complete the sentences.

This is Mr. Jackson. _____ phone number is 555-2813.

_____ address is 3317 Maple Drive.

Irma and Edgar are married. _____ phone number is 555-3765. _____ address is 1700 Burns Avenue.

F. Complete the sentences.

1. John is single. _____ address is 3215 Park Street.

2. You're a student here. _____ phone number is 555-2121, right?

3. We're from Russia. _____ address is 1652 Main Street.

4. I'm a new student. _____ name is Julie.

G. **Learn the introductions.**

This is …	This is Oscar.
Meet …	Meet Julie.
I want to introduce …	I want to introduce Edgar.

H. **Listen and circle.**

CD 1
TR 34

1. This is …   Meet …   I want to introduce …

2. This is …   Meet …   I want to introduce …

3. This is …   Meet …   I want to introduce …

INTONATION

What's your name?

What's your phone number?

What's your address?

I. **SURVEY** **Talk to four classmates.**

Name (What's your name?)	Phone number (What's your phone number?)	Address (What's your address?)
1.		
2.		
3.		
4.		

J. **Introduce a classmate to the class.**

GOAL ▒ Describe your surroundings

A. Listen and repeat. Point to the picture.

CD 1
TR 35

| trash can | file cabinets | board | bookcase | plant | door |

B. LOCATE Write: *desk, computer, chair,* and *book.*

C. Listen and point.

CD 1
TR 36

D. RELATE Ask questions. Use the words in Exercise A.

EXAMPLE: Where's the trash can?

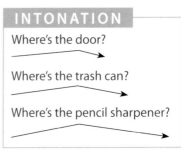

INTONATION

Where's the door?

Where's the trash can?

Where's the pencil sharpener?

E. Read.

Prepositions of Location

Where's the desk?

It's **behind** the chair.

Where's the plant?

It's **on** the desk.

Where's the trash can?

It's **between** the desk and the bookcase.

Where are the file cabinets?

They're **next to** the computer.

Where are the students?

They're **in front of** the board.

Where are the books?

They're **in** the bookcase.

F. APPLY Look at the picture in Exercise B. Ask *where is the teacher, plant,* and *trash can.* Ask *where are the file cabinets, students,* and *books.*

Student A: Where is the teacher?

Student B: He is next to the door.

Student A: Where are the file cabinets?

Student B: They are behind the computers.

G. CREATE Draw your classroom.

H. Write.

1. Where is the teacher's desk? _____

2. Where is the trash can? _____

3. Where is the board? _____

4. Where are the books? _____

5. Where are the file cabinets? _____

LESSON ③ What are you doing?

GOAL ▇ Identify common activities

🎧 **A. Listen and point to the students.**

CD 1
TR 37

B. IDENTIFY Write the names of the students.

1. listen _____

2. read _____

3. write _____

4. talk _____

C. Read the words and find examples in your classroom.

D. IDENTIFY Write the words from Exercise C.

1.
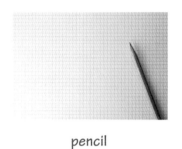

_____pencil_____

2.

_____

3.

_____

4.
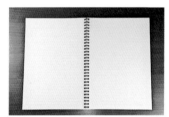

_____

5.

_____

6.

_____

7.

_____

8.

_____

9.

_____

E. CLASSIFY Complete the table with the objects in Exercise D.

Write	Listen	Read

F. Read.

Present Continuous				
He	is	read		He is reading. / She is reading.
She		write		He is writing. / She is writing.
		listen	-ing	He is listening. / She is listening.
		talk		He is talking. / She is talking.
		sit		He is sitting. / She is sitting.
		stand		He is standing. / She is standing.

G. Write.

1. _She is reading._

2. _She is listening._

3. He _____

4. He _____

5. _____

6. _____

H. REPORT Write about your classmates.

1. _Juan is sitting._

2. _____

3. _____

4. _____

5. _____

LESSON (4) When's English class?

GOAL   Plan a schedule

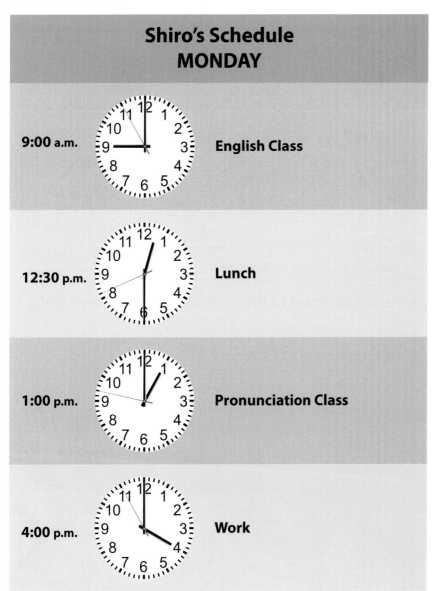

A. Read and listen.

CD 1
TR 38

**Shiro's Schedule
MONDAY**

9:00 a.m. — **English Class**

12:30 p.m. — **Lunch**

1:00 p.m. — **Pronunciation Class**

4:00 p.m. — **Work**

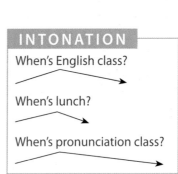

INTONATION

When's English class?

When's lunch?

When's pronunciation class?

B. IDENTIFY Look at Shiro's schedule.

1. When's English class? _It's at nine o'clock._____

2. When's lunch? _____

3. When's pronunciation class? _____

4. When's work? _____

C. What time is it? Write.

1. It's ___3:00___.

2. It's ___3:30___.

3. It's _____.

4. It's _____.

5. It's _____.

6. It's _____.

7. It's _____.

8. It's _____.

D. RELATE Practice the conversation. Point to the clocks in Exercise C and make new conversations.

Student A: What time is it? (Point to number 4 in Exercise C.)

Student B: It's <u>five thirty</u>.

It's one thirty at Grand Central Station in New York City.

E. **Listen and write.**

<table>
<tr><td colspan="2" align="center">**Julie's Schedule**
MONDAY</td></tr>
<tr><td>__9:00 a.m.__</td><td>**English Class**</td></tr>
<tr><td>_____</td><td>**Work**</td></tr>
<tr><td>_____</td><td>**Lunch**</td></tr>
<tr><td>_____</td><td>**Dinner**</td></tr>
<tr><td>_____</td><td>**Bedtime**</td></tr>
</table>

F. **Listen and read.**

Julie: When's English class?

Mr. Jackson: It's at nine o'clock.

Julie: What time is it now?

Mr. Jackson: It's seven thirty.

G. **Practice the conversation in Exercise F. Make new conversations.**

A: When's _____?

B: It's _____.

A: What time is it now?

B: It's _____.

H. **PLAN** Write your schedule on a separate piece of paper.

LESSON **5** It's cold today

A. Listen and repeat.

CD 1
TR 41

| windy | cloudy | foggy | rainy | snowy | cold | hot | sunny |

B. IDENTIFY Listen and write words from Exercise A.

CD 1
TR 42

San Francisco, United States

Montreal, Canada

Havana, Cuba
hot

Patagonia, Chile

Tokyo, Japan

New York City, United States

C. Review the weather.

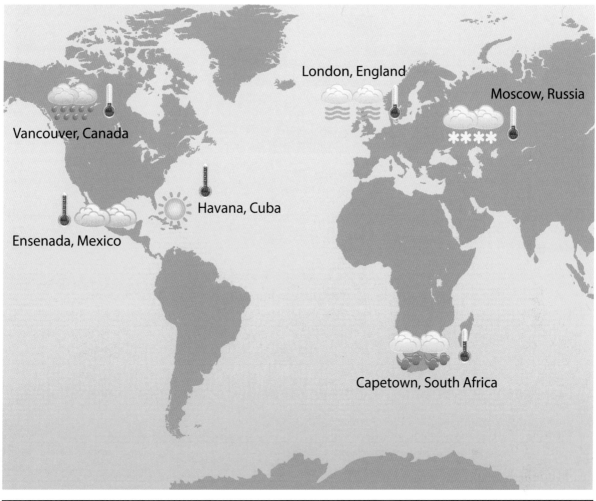

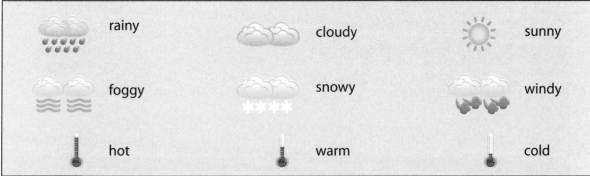

D. RELATE Practice the conversation. Use the information in Exercise C to make new conversations.

A: How's the weather in <u>Havana, Cuba</u> today?

B: It's <u>hot and sunny</u>.

E. CLASSIFY Write the correct clothes for the weather.

sandals

boots

a t-shirt

an umbrella

Rainy	Sunny

F. Read.

Simple Present		
I, You, We, They	need	I **need** an umbrella.
He, She	needs	She **needs** an umbrella.

G. Practice the conversation. Use the words below to make new conversations.

I	You	He	She	We	They

Student A: How's the weather today?
Student B: It's rainy.
Student A: He needs an umbrella.

Student A: How's the weather today?
Student B: It's sunny.
Student A: I need a t-shirt.

H. PREDICT Write the weather for the week.

Monday	Tuesday	Wednesday	Thursday	Friday	Saturday	Sunday

I. Look on the Internet or in a newspaper. Check the weather for the week and compare it with your predictions in Exercise H.

▶ **It's raining hard**

Before You Watch

A. **Look at the picture and answer the questions.**

1. Where are Hector, Mateo, and Naomi?

2. What's the weather like? How do you know?

While You Watch

B. ▶ **Watch the video and circle the words you hear.**

boots

umbrella

poncho

snowy

rainy

windy

cold

bad weather

cloudy

Check Your Understanding

C. **Put the events in order.**

1. _____ Mateo enters.

2. _____ Naomi, Hector, and Mateo run outside.

3. __1__ Hector enters.

4. _____ Naomi enters.

5. _____ Naomi, Hector, and Mateo talk about the weather.

A. Read.

Adult School Application

| Personal Information>> | Household Information | Essay | Payment | Contact Us |

Name	**Binh and Anh Duong**
Country of Origin	**Vietnam** ▼
Address	**4471 Broadway**
E-mail Address	**duong@mai1.com**
City	**Sacramento** ▼
State	**CA** ▼
Zip Code	**94203**
Phone Number	**916-555-3765**

Submit

B. Complete.

I want to introduce _____ and _____. They are from _____.

_____ address is _____.

_____ phone number is _____.

C. Ask a classmate for information. Introduce your classmate to another student.

D. Read.

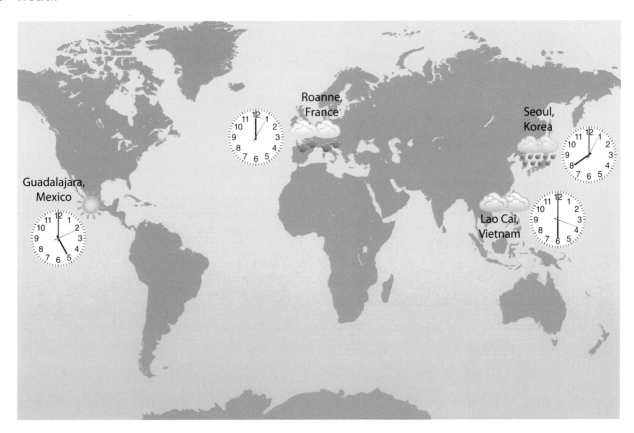

E. Write.

1. How's the weather in Korea? _It's rainy in Korea._

   What time is it? _It's 8:00._

2. How's the weather in France? _____

   What time is it? _____

3. How's the weather in Mexico? _____

   What time is it? _____

4. How's the weather in Vietnam? _____

   What time is it? _____

Learner Log

I can identify common activities.   I can describe my surroundings.

■ Yes   ■ No   ■ Maybe   ■ Yes   ■ No   ■ Maybe

F.   Match.

1.

a.   He is listening.

2.

b.   He is writing.

3.

c.   She is talking.

4.

d.   He is reading.

G.   Write.

 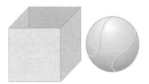 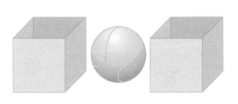 

_____in_____   _____   _____   _____

TEAM PROJECT ✓ Make a display

COLLABORATE Form a team with four or five students. In your team, you need:

Position	Job description	Student name
Student 1: Team Leader	Check that everyone speaks English. Check that everyone participates.	
Student 2: Writer	Help team members write.	
Student 3: Artist	Arrange a display with help from the team.	
Students 4/5: Spokespeople	Prepare a presentation.	

1. Draw a picture of yourself.
   Draw a map of your country.
   Draw a clock with the time in your country.
   Draw the weather in your country.

2. Present each student's work in your group to the class.

What time is it in your country?

EXPLORER JOE RIIS

A Busy Schedule

"I wake up really early in my tent ... then start my 18-hour workday of photographing wildlife and science."
—Joe Riis

A. PREDICT **Look at the picture. Answer the questions.**

1. Where is Joe? What is he doing?

2. Look at what Joe is wearing. What's the weather like?

B. **PREDICT** What time does Joe do the following activities? Put a check (✓) in the table for each question.

	10:00 p.m.	6:00 a.m.	8:00 a.m.
What time does he wake up?			
What time does he take photos?			
What time does he go to bed?			

C. Read the interview with Joe Riis.

> **Joe Riis is a wildlife photojournalist. He takes photos of wild animals and tells stories using his pictures.**
>
> **Interviewer:** Joe, you have a busy schedule, so thank you for your time. Can you tell us what you do?
>
> **Joe:** Sure. I take photos of wild animals. I share the photos with people so they can connect with the planet.
>
> **Interviewer:** What time do you wake up?
>
> **Joe:** I wake up in my tent at 6:00 a.m.
>
> **Interviewer:** What time do you take photos?
>
> **Joe:** I take photos all day! I start at 8:00 a.m.
>
> **Interviewer:** What do you do next?
>
> **Joe:** I talk with people to get information I need to tell stories with my photos.
>
> **Interviewer:** What time do you go to bed?
>
> **Joe:** I go to bed at 10:00 p.m.

D. **IDENTIFY** Circle the times. Look again at Exercise B. Is your table correct?

E. **RELATE** Complete the sentences about yourself.

1. My class is at _____.

2. I eat lunch at _____.

3. My English class is at _____.

4. I _____ at _____.

Food

People at a party enjoy meals
from a food truck.

UNIT OUTCOMES

- Identify common foods
- Express hunger
- Plan meals
- Make a shopping list
- Express preferences

Look at the photo and answer the questions.

1. What food can you buy from this food truck?
2. What's your favorite food?

GOAL ▦ Identify common foods

A. **Look at the picture. Where are the students?**

B. **RELATE** Listen and read the conversation. Use the words below to make new conversations.

CD 1
TR 43

a chicken sandwich	a tuna fish sandwich	a ham sandwich

Andre: The food looks good!
Silvina: Yes, it does.
Andre: What are you eating?
Silvina: A <u>turkey sandwich</u>.

C. IDENTIFY Listen and point.

apples	butter	eggs	milk	tomatoes
bananas	cheese	lettuce	oranges	turkey
bread	chicken	mayonnaise	potatoes	water

D. Match the letters in the picture to the food words. Write the words.

a. _____milk_____ b. _____ c. _____

d. _____ e. _____ f. _____

g. _____ h. _____ i. _____

j. _____ k. _____ l. _____

m. _____ n. _____ o. _____

E. Look and read.

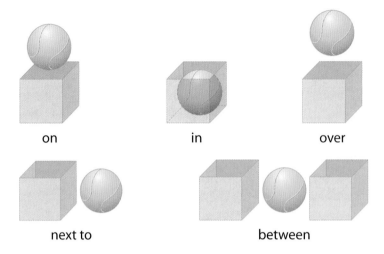

on   in   over

next to   between

F. **CLASSIFY** Look at the picture in Exercise C. Write the foods in the table.

on the counter	*in* the refrigerator	*over* the counter
bread		

G. Look at the picture in Exercise C again. Complete the sentences with *next to* or *between*.

1. The water is _____ the milk.

2. The turkey is _____ the bread and the cheese.

3. The mayonnaise is _____ the chicken.

4. The cheese is _____ the turkey and the tomatoes.

H. Practice the conversation. Use the picture in Exercise C to make new conversations.

A: Where's the <u>bread</u>?
B: It's <u>next to the turkey</u>.

I. **APPLY** Make a list of foods in your refrigerator on a sheet of paper and share it with a partner.

GOAL ▓ Express hunger

A. **Look at the picture. Where are Saul and Chen?**

🎧 **B.** **Listen and read.**

CD 1
TR 45

Saul: I'm hungry.

Chen: Me, too.

Saul: What's for dinner?

Chen: <u>Chicken and vegetables</u>.

C. **RELATE** **Practice the conversation in Exercise B. Use the meals below to make new conversations.**

chicken
sandwiches

hamburgers
and fries

tacos

rice and vegetables

D. Read about Saul and Chen. Then, read the chart.

Saul is hungry. He is not thirsty.

Chen is thirsty. He is not hungry.

Subject	Be		Example sentence
The Verb *Be*			
I	am (not)	hungry thirsty	I am (I'm) hungry. I am not (I'm not) hungry.
He	is (not)		He is (He's) thirsty. He is not (He's not) thirsty.
She			She is (She's) hungry. She is not (She's not) hungry.
We	are (not)		We are (We're) thirsty. We are not (We're not) thirsty.
You			You are (You're) hungry. You are not (You're not) hungry.
They			They are (They're) thirsty. They are not (They're not) thirsty.

E. RELATE Write. Follow the example sentences in the chart.

1. Edgar _____is_____ hungry.

   He's not thirsty. _____

2. Roselia and Thanh _____ thirsty.

   _____

3. We _____ hungry.

   _____

4. She _____ not hungry.

   _____

5. I _____ thirsty.

   _____

6. You _____ not hungry.

   _____

F. Read and listen.

CD 1
TR 46

carrots

oranges

apples

chips

cookies

milk

water

G. IDENTIFY Listen and write.

CD 1
TR 47-50

1. _____carrots_____

2. _____

3. _____

4. _____

H. Practice.

Student A: What's your favorite snack?

Student B: My favorite snack is <u>cookies</u>.

I. SURVEY Ask your classmates about their favorite snacks. Use the conversation in Exercise H.

Name	Food

LESSON 3 Let's have spaghetti!

GOAL ▌Plan meals

A. Look at the recipe. Read the ingredients.

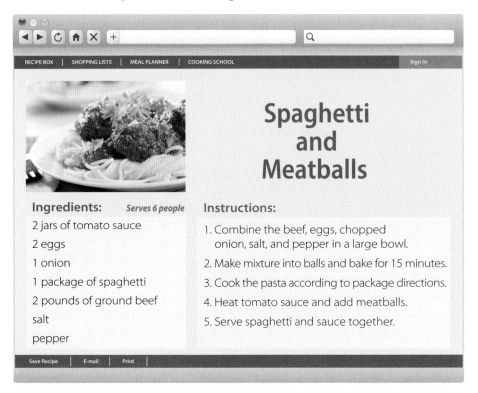

Spaghetti and Meatballs

Ingredients: *Serves 6 people*

2 jars of tomato sauce
2 eggs
1 onion
1 package of spaghetti
2 pounds of ground beef
salt
pepper

Instructions:

1. Combine the beef, eggs, chopped onion, salt, and pepper in a large bowl.
2. Make mixture into balls and bake for 15 minutes.
3. Cook the pasta according to package directions.
4. Heat tomato sauce and add meatballs.
5. Serve spaghetti and sauce together.

B. Write.

1. How many jars of tomato sauce do you need? _____ *two jars* _____

2. How many eggs do you need? _____

3. How many onions do you need? _____

4. How many packages of spaghetti do you need? _____

5. How many pounds of ground beef do you need? _____

C. IDENTIFY Listen and circle.

CD 1
TR 51-54

1. jar   package   pound

2. jar   package   pound

3. jar   package   pound

4. jar   package   pound

D. Read the chart. Listen and repeat.

Singular and Plural Nouns	
Singular	**Plural**
jar	jars
can	cans
bag	bags
package	packages
pound	pounds
Exceptions potato	potato<u>es</u>
tomato	tomato<u>es</u>
sandwich	sandwich<u>es</u>

E. **CONSTRUCT** Practice the conversation. Complete the table and make new conversations.

Student A: What do we need?
Student B: We need <u>apples</u>.

PLURALS		
/s/	/z/	/iz/
chip**s**	jar**s**	packag**es**
carrot**s**	can**s**	orang**es**

Fruit		Vegetables	
apple	/z/ apples	carrot	/s/
orange	/iz/	tomato	/z/
banana	/z/	potato	/z/
pear	/z/	pepper	/z/

F. **Write the food words and the quantities.**

four cookies

G. **RELATE** **Practice the conversation. Use the pictures to make new conversations.**

Student A: What are the ingredients?
Student B: <u>Two eggs and one onion.</u>

1.   2.   3.   4.

H. **PLAN** **Work in a group. Think of more fruits to make a fruit salad.**

Fruit Salad		
Ingredients _Serves 6 people_	_1_ banana	__ _____
	_2_ apples	__ _____
	__ pear	__ _____
	__ orange	__ _____

LESSON (4) What's for dinner?

GOAL ■ Make a shopping list

CD 1
TR 56

A. Listen and point.

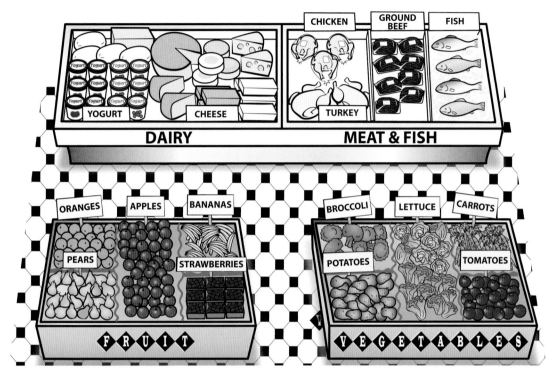

B. CLASSIFY Write the words in the correct shopping lists.

Meat and Fish	Vegetables	Fruit	Dairy
1. ground beef	1. _____	1. _____	1. _____
2. _____	2. _____	2. _____	2. _____
3. _____	3. _____	3. _____	_____
4. _____	4. _____	4. _____	_____
_____	5. _____	5. _____	_____
_____	_____	_____	_____
_____	_____	_____	_____

C. Complete the shopping lists with your own ideas.

D. Read Amadeo's shopping list.

Shopping List

apples	tomatoes
water	chicken
milk	eggs
carrots	chips
cheese	

E. **LOCATE** What does Amadeo want? Circle the items.

oranges	apples	eggs
potatoes	cheese	broccoli

F. What does Yoshi want? Listen and write.

CD 1
TR 57

Shopping List

oranges		

Farmers markets sell local food products.

G. Read.

Simple Present		
Subject	**Verb**	**Example sentence**
I, You, We, They	want	They **want** apples.
He, She	wants	She **wants** apples.
		He **wants** apples.

H. COMPARE Look at Amadeo's and Yoshi's shopping lists in exercises D and F. Complete the diagram.

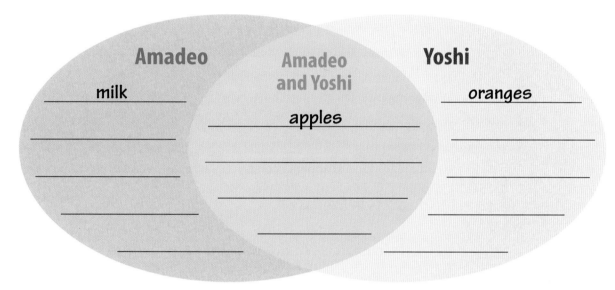

Amadeo
milk

Amadeo and Yoshi
apples

Yoshi
oranges

I. What do you want? Make a list.

Shopping List

J. What does your partner want? Ask your partner and write.

Shopping List

K. Share your partner's information with a group.

LESSON **5** What do you like?

GOAL ■ Express preferences

A. Circle the desserts you like to eat. Listen and repeat.

CD 1
TR 58

cake

pie

ice cream

yogurt

cookies

bar of chocolate

bag of candy

B. Listen and point to the desserts in Exercise A.

CD 1
TR 59–61

C. RANK Number the desserts in Exercise A. Number 1 is your favorite.

cake   _____

pie   _____

ice cream   _____

yogurt   _____

cookies   _____

chocolate   _____

candy   _____

D. Listen and take notes. Write what Maria likes.

CD 1
TR 62

1. Maria likes _____.

2. She likes _____.

3. She likes _____.

E. Read the chart.

Simple Present		
Subject	**Verb**	**Example sentence**
I, You, We, They	like	I **like** ice cream.
	eat	We **eat** ice cream.
	want	They **want** ice cream.
He, She	likes	She **likes** chocolate.
	eats	He **eats** chocolate.
	wants	She **wants** chocolate.

F. Write the verb.

1. I _____ (want) apple pie.

2. Maria _____ *likes* _____ (like) ice cream.

3. You _____ (eat) pie.

4. They _____ (eat) cookies.

5. We _____ (like) fruit.

6. Saul _____ (like) candy.

7. We _____ (want) yogurt.

8. I _____ (like) _____.

G. IDENTIFY Write about the pictures.

1. _She wants cookies._____ 2. _____ 3. _____

H. Read.

Student A: Do you like <u>ice cream</u> for dessert?
Student B: No, I like <u>pie</u>.

I. Practice the conversation in Exercise H. Use the words in Exercise A to make new conversations.

J. COMPARE What desserts does your partner like? Complete the diagram.

I like ...
_____
_____
_____
_____
_____
_____
_____
_____

My partner and I like ...
_____
_____
_____
_____
_____
_____
_____

My partner likes ...
_____
_____
_____
_____
_____
_____
_____

K. Tell your classmates about your partner.

▶ # What's for lunch?

Before You Watch

A. Look at the picture and answer the questions.

1. Where are Hector and Mateo?

2. What do you think they are going to eat?

While You Watch

B. ▶ Watch the video and circle what Hector and Mateo order.

Mateo	Hector
1. a. chicken soup b. chicken salad	4. a. taco b. cheeseburger
2. a. iced coffee b. iced tea	5. a. fried rice b. French fries
3. a. apple pie b. chocolate cake	6. a. onion rings b. chicken salad

Check Your Understanding

C. Match the questions to the answers.

Server	Customer
1. How are you? 2. Do you need some more time to look at the menu? 3. What would you like? 4. Do you want something to drink? 5. Would you like anything for dessert?	a. Chocolate cake for me, please. b. No, I'm ready to order. c. I'll have the special. d. Great. I'm really hungry. e. Yes, I'll have an iced tea with no sugar.

Review

A. Write the food words.

_____

_____

_____

_____

_____

_____

B. Write the plural food words.

Singular	Plural
apple	
orange	
chicken	
banana	
cookie	
egg	
chip	
potato	
tomato	
carrot	

C. Write *am, is,* or *are.*

1. Maria _____ thirsty.

2. Kim and David _____ not hungry.

3. Lan and Mai _____ hungry.

4. Rafael _____ not thirsty.

5. Colby _____ hungry.

6. Marco and Eva _____ thirsty.

7. Lara _____ not hungry.

8. I _____ thirsty.

D. Write negative sentences.

1. Eric is hungry.   He's not thirsty. _____

2. Maria is thirsty.   _____

3. Saul and Chen are hungry. _____

4. I am thirsty.   _____

E. Write the simple present.

1. Chrissy _____ (like) hamburgers.

2. You _____ (eat) tacos.

3. Laura _____ (want) vegetables.

4. Rosie and Amadeo _____ (like) rice.

5. We _____ (eat) fish and chicken.

6. They _____ (want) pie.

7. Karl _____ (like) oranges.

8. I _____.

Learner Log

I can make a shopping list.   I can plan meals.

■ Yes   ■ No   ■ Maybe   ■ Yes   ■ No   ■ Maybe

F.   **Talk to two classmates. Ask:** *What do you want?*

Shopping List   Shopping List

_____   _____

_____   _____

_____   _____

_____   _____

_____   _____

G.   **Read the lists in Exercise F. Write.**

Singular Foods	Plural Foods
_____	_____
_____	_____
_____	_____
_____	_____
_____	_____
_____	_____
_____	_____
_____	_____

✓ # Make a shopping list

1. COLLABORATE Form a team with four or five students. In your team, you need:

Position	Job description	Student name
Student 1: Team Leader	Check that everyone speaks English. Check that everyone participates.	
Student 2: Writer	Write food names.	
Student 3: Artist	Draw pictures for the shopping list with help from the team.	
Students 4/5: Spokespeople	Prepare a presentation.	

2. You are a family. What is your last name?

3. Make a shopping list with food from this unit.

4. Draw pictures of the food on your list.

5. Present your list to the class.

Shopping lists are different in other parts of the world.

EXPLORER CATHERINE JAFFEE

A Recipe for Success

"...become involved in what you eat, grow, and plant, and make an effort to connect with other people ..."
—Catherine Jaffee

A. PREDICT Look at the picture. Answer the questions.

1. What are the people in the picture wearing?

2. What food do you think the article will be about? Why?

3. Do you think Catherine likes her job? Why?

Some kinds of honey bees are disappearing. Balyolu helps the Caucasian honey bee to survive.

B. FIND OUT Circle the correct answers.

1. A *project* is a . . .

    a. plan of work.

    b. vacation.

2. A *leader* is a person who . . .

    a. guides others.

    b. makes honey.

3. *An expert* is a person who . . .

    a. knows a little.

    b. knows a lot.

4. *Beekeepers* are people who . . .

    a. work with people.

    b. work with bees.

C. Read about Catherine Jaffee.

Catherine Jaffee is a food *expert*. She has a very important job. She helps communities to be successful through food. Balyolu—one of Catherine's projects—helps *beekeepers* in Turkey to make honey and teaches them how to be business *leaders*. This *project* also helps to care for bees.

Some people put honey in yogurt; some people put it on their toast. However you use honey, Catherine is working to make sure it stays on your shopping list.

D. CLASSIFY Complete the chart about the story.

Person	Food	Insect	Place
Catherine Jaffee			

E. Read the shopping list.

Summer Salad with Honey

1 package of spinach

1 cup of strawberries

1 small onion

1/2 cup of blueberries

1/4 cup of cheese

honey

F. APPLY Find a meal that contains honey. Write a shopping list.

UNIT 4

Clothing

Clothing comes in
many different styles
and colors.

UNIT OUTCOMES

- Identify types of clothing
- Ask for and give directions in a store
- Describe clothing
- Make purchases
- Read advertisements

Look at the photo and answer the questions.

1. What types of clothing can you see?
2. What colors are the clothes?

LESSON **1** **What's on sale?**

GOAL   Identify types of clothing

 A. **IDENTIFY** **Listen and point to the clothing.**

B. **Listen to the conversation and read.**

Salesperson: May I help you?
Maria: Yes, I want a shirt, pants, a sweater, and shoes.

C. **Read the conversation in Exercise B again. Write sentences.**

1. _She wants a shirt._ _____.

2. _____.

3. _____.

4. _____.

D. IDENTIFY What clothes can you see in the ad?

E. Listen and write the number of the conversation.

CD 1 TR 65

____ _____

____ _____

> **A PAIR OF ...**
>
> Use *a pair of* with clothes that have two parts (socks, gloves). *A pair of* can also be used with clothes that have two legs (pants, shorts).

____ _____

1 _____blouse_____

____ _____

____ _____

____ _____

____ _____

F. Write the types of clothing for each picture in Exercise E.

~~blouse~~   socks   dress   shirt   pants   sweater   coat   shorts

G. Read.

Simple Present: *Have*		
Subject	*Have*	**Example sentence**
I, You, We, They	have	I **have** two shirts. I **have** a pair of socks.
He, She	has	She **has** a dress. She **has** a pair of shoes.

H. Write.

1. (blouse)   She <u>has a blouse</u>.

   (shoes)   He <u>has shoes</u>. **or** He <u>has a pair of shoes</u>.

2. (dress)   She _____.

3. (coats)   They _____.

4. (socks)   I _____. **or** I _____.

5. (sweaters)   We _____.

6. (pants)   You _____. **or** You _____.

I. What's in Maria's closet? Write.

3 _____

1 pair of _____

1 _____

J. LIST What's in your closet? Write four items.

_____   _____

_____   _____

LESSON 2 Where's the fitting room?

GOAL ▦ Ask for and give directions in a store

A. Listen and point.

CD 1
TR 66

B. CLASSIFY Look at the picture in Exercise A and write the clothes.

Men's	Women's	Children's	Teen Boys'	Teen Girls'
		hats		skirts

Lesson 2 **89**

C. Read.

Prepositions of Location	
a. It's **in the front of** the store. b. It's **in the corner of** the store. c. It's **in the middle of** the store. d. It's **in the back of** the store. e. It's **on the left side of** the store. f. It's **on the right side of** the store.	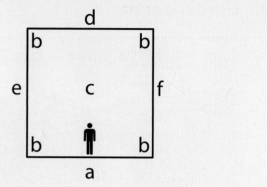

D. Look at the picture in Exercise A. Answer the questions.

1. Where's the fitting room? *It's in the back of the store.* _____

2. Where's the men's section? _____

3. Where's the women's section? _____

4. Where's the children's section? _____

5. Where's the teen boys' section? _____

6. Where's the teen girls' section? _____

E. RELATE Listen and practice the conversation. Make new conversations. (Student A looks at Exercise D and Student B looks at the picture in Exercise A.)

CD 1
TR 67

Student A: Can you help me?
Student B: Sure. What can I do for you?
Student A: Where's the <u>fitting room?</u>
Student B: It's <u>in the back of the store.</u>
Student A: Thank you.

F. Listen and point.

CD 1
TR 68

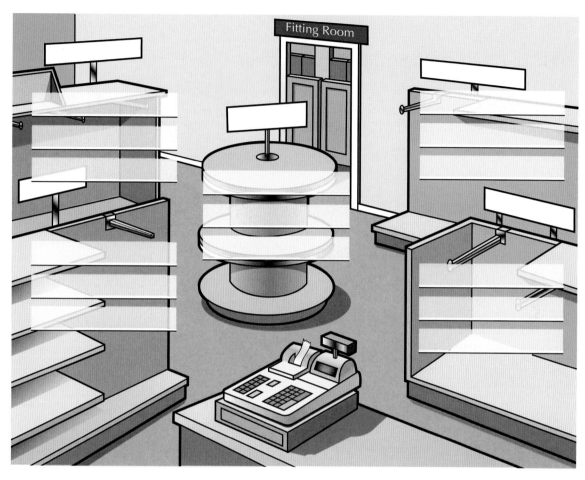

Fitting Room

G. Listen and write the sections in the picture.

CD 1
TR 69

H. **CREATE** In a group, write clothing in the picture for each section.

The men's section of a clothing store

LESSON **3** **What colors do you like?**

GOAL ▪ Describe clothing

A. INFER Look at the picture. What is Yusuf doing?

CD 1
TR 70

B. Listen and read.

Salesperson:	Can I help you?
Yusuf:	Yes, I want a shirt.
Salesperson:	What color do you like—white, blue, or red?
Yusuf:	I don't know, maybe blue.

YES/NO QUESTIONS

Can I help you?

May I help you?

Do you need help?

C. Listen and repeat. Read the colors in the picture.

CD 1
TR 71

white — green —

black
purple

pink

blue
yellow

gray —
orange —

brown

red —

ADJECTIVE POSITION

A blue tie (correct)

A tie blue (not correct)

D. Listen and point to the clothing items.

CD 1
TR 72

| **S = Small** | **M = Medium** | **L = Large** | **XL = Extra Large** |

E. CLASSIFY Look at Exercise D. Complete the inventory.

Adel's Inventory List			
Quantity (How many?)	**Item**	**Size**	**Color**
	shirt	S	
2	shirt	M	
1	shirt		
2	shirt		

F. Read.

Singular	Plural
There **is** one green shirt. There**'s** one green shirt.	There **are** two black shirts.

G. Practice the conversation. Use the information in Exercise E to make new conversations.

Student A: How many <u>white</u> shirts are there?
Student B: There's <u>one</u>.

H. **CREATE** Write an inventory for your class. Write about your classmates' clothing.

Class Inventory		
Quantity (How many?)	Item	Color

I. **CREATE** Write an inventory of the clothes in your closet.

LESSON 4 That's $5.00

A. IDENTIFY Listen and point to the cash registers.

CD 1
TR 73

1.

2.

3.

B. Circle the correct number from Exercise A.

1. one dollar	1	2	3
2. ten dollars and forty-one cents	1	2	3
3. six dollars and twenty-five cents	1	2	3

C. Listen and read with your teacher.

CD 1
TR 74

a dollar bill	a dollar coin $1.00	a quarter $.25	a dime $.10	a nickel $.05	a penny $.01

D. RELATE Match the amounts with the money.

1. $.50

a.

2. $15.08

b.

3. $35.10

c.

E. Practice the conversations with a partner.

Student A: How much is the shirt?
Student B: It's $15.00.
Student A: Thanks.

Student A: How much are the shorts?
Student B: They're $10.41.
Student A: Thanks.

F. Study the chart.

Singular	Plural
How much **is** the dress?	How much **are** the shoes?

G. **Listen and write.**

CD 1
TR 75-80

1.

_$32.50_

3.

_____

5.

_____

2.

_____

4.

_____

6.

_____

H. **CONFIRM** **Ask a classmate for the prices in Exercise G. Write the receipts.**

Adel's
Clothing Emporium

pants $32.50

Total $32.50

Customer Copy

Adel's
Clothing Emporium

shirt ..... _____
shoes .... _____

Total .... _____

Customer Copy

Adel's
Clothing Emporium

dress ..... _____
shorts .... _____
blouse .... _____

Total .... _____

Customer Copy

I. **CREATE** **Speak to a partner. Ask for three items and complete the receipt.**

Student A: How can I help you?
Student B: How much <u>are the pants</u>?
Student A: <u>$32.50</u>
Student B: Thanks. I want <u>two pairs</u>.
Student A: Great. Anything else?

Adel's
Clothing Emporium

_____ _____
_____ _____
_____ _____

Total .... _____

Customer Copy

GOAL ▧ Read advertisements

🎧 **A. Read, listen, and write.**
CD 1
TR 81

adel's
clothing emporium

B. Write.

1. How much are the shirts? $22.50

2. How much are the dresses?   _____

3. How much are the shoes?   _____

4. How much are the pants?   _____

C. RELATE Ask a classmate the questions in Exercise B.

D. Read.

How much and How many		
Question		**Answer**
How much	(money) is the sweater?	$33.00.
How much	is the shirt?	The shirt is $23.00.
How much	are the shoes?	They are / They're $40.00.
How many	coats do you want?	I want three coats.
How many	shirts do you want?	I want two shirts.

E. Practice the conversation. Use the information in Exercise A to make new conversations.

Student A: Can I help you?
Student B: Yes, I want <u>shirts</u>.
Student A: How many shirts do you want?
Student B: I want two shirts. How much are they?
Student A: They are <u>$22.50</u> each.

F. CLASSIFY Practice the conversation in Exercise E again. Speak to your classmates and take orders. (Use the ad in Exercise A.)

Name	Quantity (How many?)	Product	Price
Yusuf	two	shirts	$22.50

G. Read.

NORMA'S
FINE CLOTHING

SAVE $8.00 — $24.00 ALL SIZES

$20.00 ALL SIZES

$35.00 ALL SIZES

SALE $35.00 ALL SIZES

SAVE $12.00 — $35.00 SIZES 6 - 12

SALE $16.00 ALL SIZES

H. COMPARE Look at the ads for Norma's Fine Clothing and Adel's Clothing Emporium (Exercise A). Write the prices.

	Norma's Fine Clothing	Adel's Clothing Emporium
shirt	$24.00	$22.50
pants		
shoes		
dress		
sweater		

I. CREATE In a group, make an advertisement for a new clothing store. Practice the conversation from Exercise E.

LIFESKILLS ▶ That's a good deal

Before You Watch

A. Look at the picture and answer the questions.

1. Where are Hector and Mr. Sanchez?

2. What is Hector holding?

While You Watch

B. ▶ Watch the video and fill in the missing prices.

Item	Regular price	Sale price
jacket	$160	
coat		
pants		
tie		
shirt		

Check Your Understanding

C. Put the sentences in order to make a conversation.

a. _____ Clerk: What color?

b. _____ Customer: Yes, I need a new tie.

c. _____ Customer: That's nice. I'll take it.

d. _____1_____ Clerk: May I help you?

e. _____ Clerk: How about this one?

f. _____ Customer: Blue. It's for a job interview.

Review

Learner Log

I can identify types of clothing.   I can describe clothing.
▇ Yes ▇ No ▇ Maybe   ▇ Yes ▇ No ▇ Maybe

A. Write the types of clothing.

1.
_____

2.
_____

3.
_____

4.
_____

5.
_____

6.
_____

7.
_____

8.
_____

B. Read and write.

1. We need three blue shirts. They are $18.59 each.

2. We need five green sweaters. They are $22.50 each.

3. We need one pair of black shoes. They are $33.00.

4. We need two red coats. They are $85.00 each.

Adel's Clothing Emporium			
Quantity (How many?)	Item	Color	Price
1.			$55.77
2.			$112.50
3.			$33.00
4.			$170.00

Learner Log

I can ask for and give directions in a store.   I can make purchases.

☐ Yes ☐ No ☐ Maybe   ☐ Yes ☐ No ☐ Maybe

C.   Write the locations.

a. _It's in the corner of the store._

b. _____

c. _____

d. _____

e. _____

f. _____

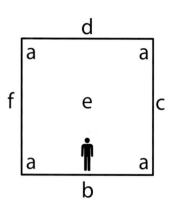

D.   Which possible bills and coins do you need? Write.

Total	$20 bills	$10 bills	$5 bills	$1 bills	Quarters	Dimes	Nickels	Pennies
$69.00								
$22.50	1			2	2			
$56.90								
$132.00								
$153.75								
$113.80								

The Lincoln Memorial can be found
on the back of the U.S. five-dollar bill.

E.   Read the ad.

F.   Write the information from the ad.

Item	Price	Savings
gray pants	$28.50	$5.00
jeans		
shirts		
blouses		
socks		
jackets		

✓ **Open a clothing store**

1. **COLLABORATE** Form a team with four or five students. In your team, you need:

Position	Job description	Student name
Student 1: Team Leader	Check that everyone speaks English. Check that everyone participates.	
Student 2: Writer	Make an inventory list.	
Student 3: Artist	Make an ad for a clothing store.	
Students 4/5: Spokespeople	Prepare a presentation.	

2. Make an ad.

3. Open a store. What is the name? Design the store.

4. Write an inventory list.

5. Present your store to the class.

The grand opening of a new store usually involves cutting a ribbon.

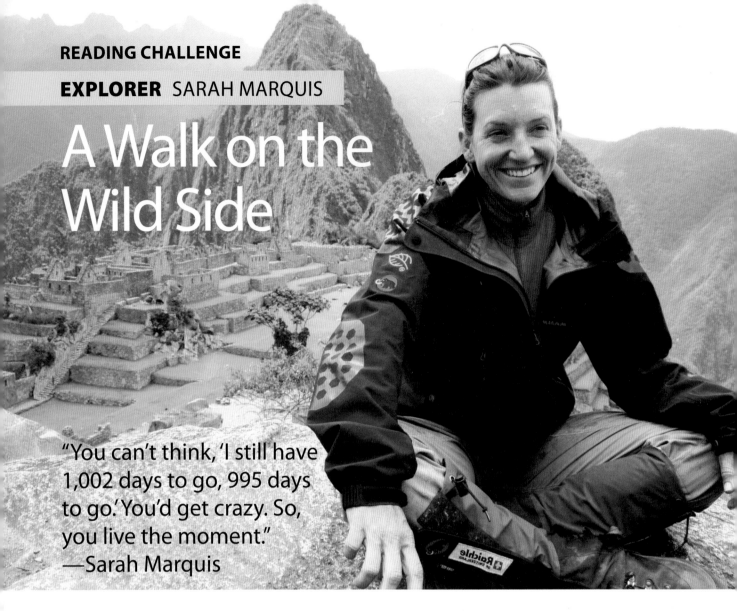

A Walk on the Wild Side

"You can't think, 'I still have 1,002 days to go, 995 days to go.' You'd get crazy. So, you live the moment."
—Sarah Marquis

A. PREDICT Look at the picture. Answer the questions.

1. Where is Sarah Marquis in the picture? What is she doing?

2. What clothes is she wearing? Why?

B. CLASSIFY Write the clothes people wear when it is hot and cold.

Hot	Cold

C. **Read about Sarah Marquis.**

Sarah Marquis is from Switzerland. She is an explorer who travels around the world *by foot*. In 2014, she was named as one of National Geographic's Adventurers of the Year for her walk from Siberia to Australia. She completed the journey in three years! After each adventure Sarah shares her stories. She walks in places like Siberia, Mongolia, and the Andes mountains in Peru. To explore cold countries like Canada, she has pants, sweaters, and coats. To explore warm countries like Australia, she has t-shirts. No matter where she goes, she always has her most important item of clothing—her shoes!

* by foot = to walk

D. **IDENTIFY** **Underline the clothing in the story.**

E. **Scan the article and write the places Sarah has explored on the map.**

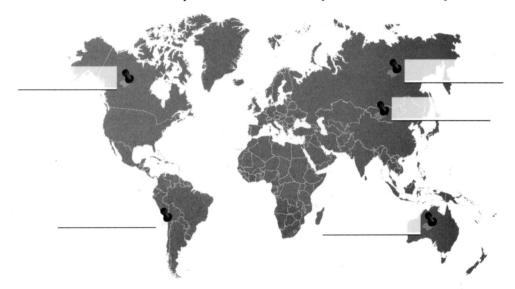

F. **Read the article again. Answer the questions.**

1. Where is it hot? _____

2. Where is it cold? _____

G. **APPLY** **Complete the sentences about you and share with a partner.**

1. I live in _____.

2. It is _____ (cold/warm/hot) most of the time.

3. I wear _____ a lot.

4. My favorite clothes are _____.

A Mongolian Family

Mongolian families move their
gers from place to place.

Over the last four units, you have met a lot of new people. You know their names, where they come from, and where they live. You may even know a little bit about their hometowns. Now you will meet a new group of people from Mongolia; however, something is different about these people. They don't always live in the same place.

Before You Watch

WORD FOCUS

A *ger* is a large, round tent used as a home by some people in Mongolia.

The *country* is a quiet place where people live outside the city.

A. What do you see in a city? What do you see in the country? Write the words in the table.

taxi	goats	farm	clothing store	farmer
house	cows	horse	bus	apartment

City	Country

B. Complete the table with your own ideas.

C. How much do you know about country living? Read the sentences and write *T* for true and *F* for false.

1. Families work together to take care of a farm. _____

2. Families live together in small apartments. _____

3. There are a lot of restaurants in the country. _____

4. Cows, goats, and horses live in the country. _____

5. It is easy to find a taxi outside the city. _____

D. **You are going to watch a video about Ochkhuu and his family. Read the words and complete the paragraph.**

> **parents:** people who have children   **mother:** a woman who has a child
>
> **wife:** a married woman   **father:** a man who has a child
>
> **daughter:** a girl child

Ochkhuu is married. He and his _____, Norvoo, have a _____. Her name is Anuka. She is six years old. Ochkhuu and his family live close to Norvoo's _____ in the country. They all live in large *gers*. Norvoo's _____ is a farmer. He is 65 years old. Norvoo's _____ is also 65 years old. Her name is Chantsal.

While You Watch

A. **Watch the video. Circle the items you see.**

supermarket	houses	calendar
school	cars	classroom
ger	shops	clothing store
TV	goats	plants

B. **Watch the video again. Circle the correct clothing.**

1. Jaya wears a white hat / coat on the farm.
2. Anuka is wearing a pink and white dress / sweater.
3. Chantsal wears a brown dress / shirt.
4. Ochkhuu wears a striped shirt / hat in the city.
5. Ochkhuu wears blue shoes / pants on the family's farm.

C. **Put the events in order. Write the correct number on the line.**

_____ a. Ochkhuu is standing on a city street.

_____ b. Anuka is sitting on the bed with her family.

_____ c. Jaya is picking up plants on the farm.

_____ d. Ochkhuu is cutting plants on the farm.

_____ e. Ochkhuu is going inside his *ger* in the city.

After You Watch

A. Complete each sentence. Write the correct word on the line.

brother	mother	father	wife	daughter

1. Chantsal is Jaya's _____.
2. Anuka is Ochkhuu's _____.
3. Jaya is Norvoo's _____.
4. Anuka does not have a _____.
5. Chantsal is Norvoo's _____.

B. Read the sentences. Circle *T* for true and *F* for false. Correct the false sentences in your notebook.

1. Ochkhuu lives in the city.   T   F
2. Mongolian *gers* are in the city and in the country. T   F
3. Anuka is 10 years old.   T   F
4. Ulaanbaatar is a city with taxis and many shops.   T   F
5. Norvoo and Jaya are 70 years old.   T   F

C. Work with a partner. What type of clothing do people wear in the country? Is it different from what people wear in the city?

EXAMPLE: In the city, men wear suits. In the country, they wear shorts and t-shirts.

Ochkhuu and his daughter, Anuka, watch a video inside a *ger*.

Our Community

Children and adults enjoy playing in a water fountain.

UNIT OUTCOMES

☐ Identify and ask about locations

☐ Describe housing

☐ Identify types of transportation

☐ Express personal information

☐ Give and follow directions

Look at the photo and answer the questions.

1. What are the people doing? Why?

2. Where can you enjoy spending time in your community?

GOAL ▮ Identify and ask about locations

A. **Look at the pictures. What types of stores do you see?**

1.

2.

3.

4.

5.

6.

B. **Listen and point.**

CD 2
TR 1

C. **Listen and write the number of the conversation.**

CD 2
TR 2–5

_____1_____ supermarket   _____ pharmacy

_____ shoe store   _____ clothing store

E. **CLASSIFY** Write the places in the table.

Place to sleep	Places to eat	Places to buy things
		clothing store

F. What other places can you think of in your community. Talk to your partner.

G. Read.

Yes/No Questions	
Question	**Answer**
Do you buy clothing at a department store?	Yes, I do.
Do you buy food at a supermarket?	No, I don't.
Do you buy shoes at a shoe store?	

H. Practice the conversations. Use the stores in Exercise A to make new conversations.

Latifa:	Chen, do you buy medicine at a pharmacy?
Chen:	Yes, I do.
Latifa:	Which one?
Chen:	Save-A-Lot Pharmacy.

James:	Do you work at a shoe store?
Trang:	No, I don't. I work at a clothing store.
James:	Which one?
Trang:	Norma's Fine Clothing.

YES/NO QUESTIONS

Do you buy shoes at a shoe store?

Do you buy food at a supermarket?

I. SURVEY Ask classmates where they buy clothes and food. Write.

Name	Clothes	Food
Peter	Norma's Fine Clothing	El Marco Restaurant

LESSON **2** **Where do you live?**

GOAL   Describe housing

A. Look at the map. Write.

a house	a mobile home	an apartment

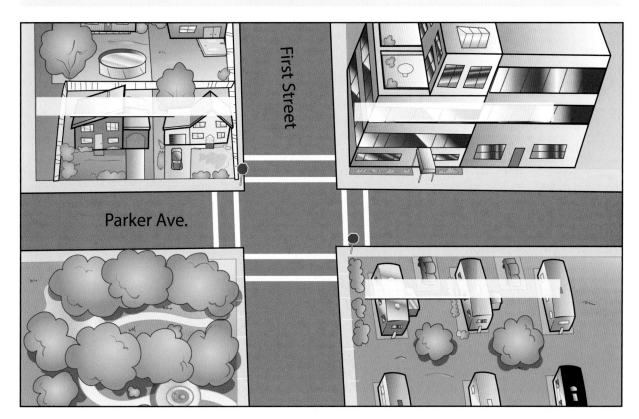

First Street

Parker Ave.

> **ON / IN**
>
> I live **on** First Street. / I live **on** Parker Avenue.
>
> I live **in** a house. / I live **in** <u>an</u> apartment.

B. Listen and practice.

Student A: Where do you live?
Student B: I live on <u>First Street</u>.
Student A: Do you live in a house or an apartment?
Student B: I live in <u>a house</u>.

C. Read.

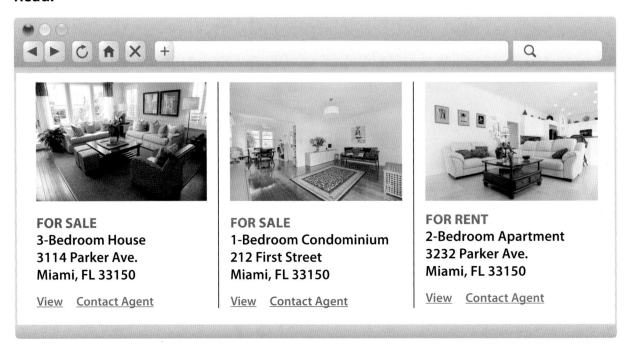

FOR SALE
3-Bedroom House
3114 Parker Ave.
Miami, FL 33150

View   Contact Agent

FOR SALE
1-Bedroom Condominium
212 First Street
Miami, FL 33150

View   Contact Agent

FOR RENT
2-Bedroom Apartment
3232 Parker Ave.
Miami, FL 33150

View   Contact Agent

D. COMPARE Check (✓) the correct answer.

1. Which home is at 3114 Parker Ave.?

☐ the house

☐ the apartment

☐ the condo

2. Which home has only one bedroom?

☐ the apartment

☐ the house

☐ the condominium

3. Which home is for sale?

☐ the apartment

☐ the condominium

☐ the house and the condo

4. Which home is for rent?

☐ the apartment

☐ the house

☐ the house and the apartment

E. Listen and write.

CD 2
TR 8

a house   an apartment   a mobile home

1. _____   2. _____   3. _____

F. **Listen and read.**

1. I'm Chen.
   I'm from China.
   I live in a house.
   I live on First Street
   in Alpine City.

2. I'm Latifa.
   I'm from Saudi Arabia.
   I live in an apartment.
   I live in Casper Town
   on Parker Avenue.

3. I'm Natalia.
   I'm from Guatemala.
   I live in a condominium
   in Alpine City on
   First Street.

G. **Practice the conversation.**

Chen: Hi, I'm <u>Chen</u>.

Latifa: Nice to meet you, <u>Chen</u>. I'm <u>Latifa</u>.

Chen: Where do you live?

Latifa: I live in <u>Casper Town</u>.

Chen: Do you live in an apartment, a condominium, or a house?

Latifa: I live in <u>an apartment</u>.

H. **Write a conversation. Change the underlined words in the conversation in Exercise G.**

Latifa: Hi, I'm Latifa. _____

Natalia: Nice to meet you, Latifa. I'm Natalia. _____

Latifa: _____

Natalia: _____

Latifa: _____

Natalia: _____

I. **CREATE** On a separate piece of paper, write and practice a conversation about you and a partner.

LESSON ③ I take the bus

GOAL ▓ Identify types of transportation

~~car~~	bicycle	taxi	train	bus

A. Write the words.

car _____

_____

_____

_____

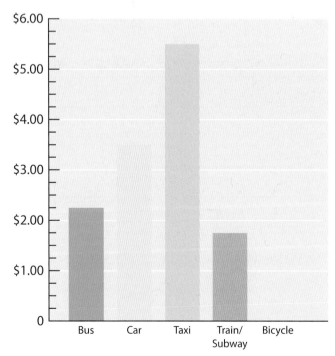

_____

B. INTERPRET Read the bar graph.

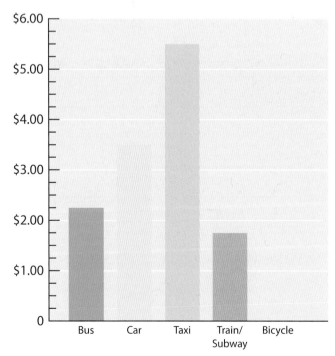

C. Practice the conversation. Use the types of transportation in Exercise A to make new conversations.

Student A: How much is it to go by bus?

Student B: $2.25.

D. Look at the map. What's the distance between Casper Town and Alpine City?

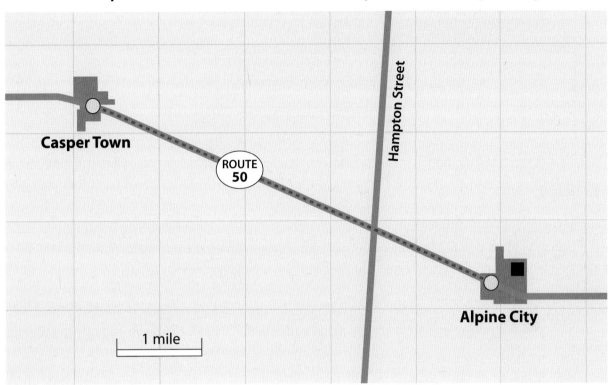

E. Listen and read.

CD 2
TR 10

Chen: Do you drive to school?
Latifa: No, I don't. <u>I take the bus</u>.
Chen: How much is it?
Latifa: It's $3.50.

F. Practice the conversation in Exercise E. Use the phrases below to make new conversations.

drive a car	take a bus
ride a bike	take a train
walk	take a taxi

G. Complete the table. Ask your classmates.

Name	Do you drive to school?

H. Read.

come / get and go / get			
		At school	**At home**
How	come / get	How do you **come / get** to school?	How do you **come / get** home?
	go / get	How do you **go / get** home?	How do you **go / get** to school?
When	come / get	When do you **come / get** to school?	When do you **come / get** home?
	go	When do you **go** home?	When do you **go** to school?

I. Practice the conversation. Make new conversations.

Latifa: How do you get to school?
Natalia: I <u>drive</u>.
Latifa: When do you go home?
Natalia: I go home at <u>3:00</u>.

J. SURVEY Ask four classmates.

Name	How do you get to school?	When do you go home?
Natalia	drive	3:00

LESSON **4** She takes the train

GOAL ▌ Express personal information

A. Listen and write.

1. I'm James.
   I'm from the U.S.
   I live in a house.
   I take the _____
   to school.

2. I'm An.
   I'm from Vietnam.
   I live in a house.
   I _____ my bike
   to school.

3. I'm Carina.
   I'm from Cuba.
   I live in an
   _____.
   I drive to school.

B. Write.

Name	Country	Housing	Transportation
James			
An			
Carina			

C. **COMPARE** Look at the information for James and An. Complete the diagram.

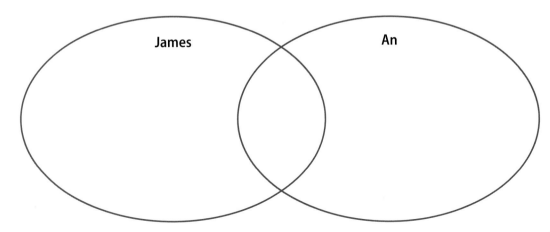

James   An

D. Read.

Simple Present		
Subject	Verb	Example sentence
I, You, We, They	live take ride walk	I **live** in Mexico. We **take** the bus. You **ride** a bicycle. They **walk** to school.
He, She, It	live**s** take**s** ride**s** walk**s**	She **lives** in Mexico He **takes** the bus. She **rides** a bicycle. She **walks** to school.

E. Write about James, Carina, and An.

1. James _____lives_____ in a house.

2. He _____ the bus to school.

3. Carina _____ in an apartment.

4. She _____ to school.

5. An _____ in a house.

6. She _____ a bicycle to school.

7. James and An _____ in a house.

F. Write about Leslie and Briana.

1. Leslie and Briana _____ in Cambodia.

2. Leslie _____ the bus to work every day.

3. Briana _____ a car to work.

4. They _____ in a house.

G. Read.

Simple Present: Verb *Be*		
Subject	**Verb *Be***	**Example sentence**
I	am	I **am** An.
He, She, It	is	She **is** from China.
We, You, They	are	They **are** married.

H. Read the chart.

Name	Country	Housing	Transportation to school
James	United States	house	bus
Latifa	Saudi Arabia	apartment	bus

I. Write.

1. James _____ is _____ from the United States.

2. James _____ in a house.

3. He _____ the bus.

4. Latifa _____ from Saudi Arabia.

5. She _____ in an apartment.

6. James and Latifa _____ the bus.

J. APPLY Answer the questions.

1. What's your name?

   My name _____ .

2. Where are you from?

   I _____ from

   _____ .

3. Do you live in a house?

   I _____ in a(n)

   _____ .

4. How do you get to school?

   I _____ to school.

GOAL ▍ Give and follow directions

A. Point to the bank, the post office, and the hospital.

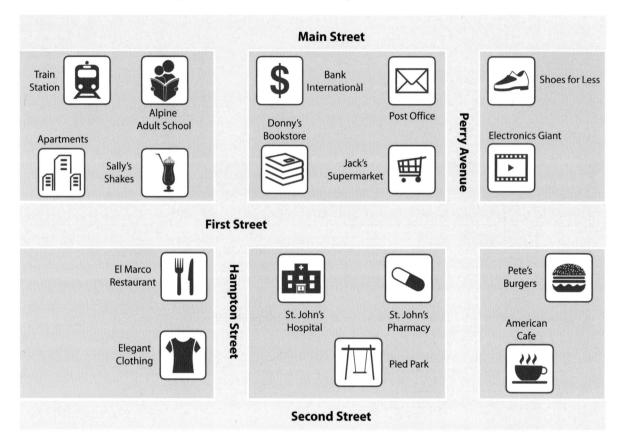

THE

the post office = Alpine City Post Office

the supermarket = Jack's Supermarket

B. Match. Draw a line.

1. Where is the adult school?

2. Where is the electronics store?

3. Where is the bookstore?

4. Where is the post office?

a. It's on Perry Avenue next to Shoes for Less.

b. It's on First Street next to the supermarket.

c. It's on Main Street next to the bank.

d. It's on Hampton Street next to Sally's Shakes.

🎧 **C.** **Listen and repeat.**

stop	go straight	turn right	turn left

D. **Write the correct words.**

turn left
_____

_____

_____

_____

E. Use the map in Exercise A to complete the directions. Start on First Street in front of Jack's Supermarket.

Give directions to the adult school.

1. _____ on First Street.

2. _____ on Hampton Street.

Give directions to the post office.

1. _____ on First Street.

2. _____ on Hampton Street.

3. _____ on Main Street.

F. Write directions to the train station.

_____

_____

_____

_____

🎧 **G.** **Listen and read.**

CD 2
TR 13

Latifa: Excuse me, where's American Café?

An: It's on Perry Avenue.

Latifa: Can you give me directions?

An: Yes. Go straight on First Street. Turn right on Perry Avenue. It's next to Pete's Burgers.

🎧 **H.** **Listen and follow the directions. Number the locations 1–4.**

CD 2
TR 14

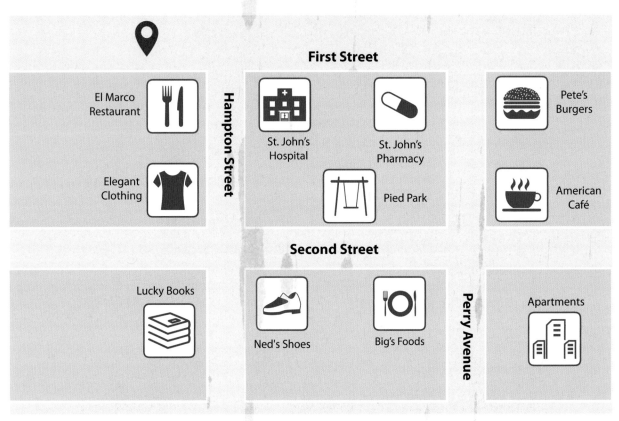

I. **Write three stores in your community.**

1. _____   2. _____   3. _____

J. **CREATE** In a group, write directions to a store from your school.

_____

_____

_____

_____

LIFESKILLS ▶ Do you live around here?

Before You Watch

A. Look at the picture and answer the questions.

1. Where are Naomi and Hector?

2. What is Hector doing?

While You Watch

B. ▶ Watch the video and complete the dialog. Use the words in the box.

bus	town	near	streets	~~live~~	going

Naomi: I (1) _____ live _____ on Maple Street.

Hector: Maple Street. That's (2) _____ Chestnut Street, isn't it?

Naomi: I think so. I'm still learning the names of all the (3) _____. I just moved here.

Mateo: Glendale's a small (4) _____. You'll get used to it pretty soon.

Naomi: I hope so. Where are you (5) _____?

Hector: I'm taking the (6) _____ to school.

Check Your Understanding

C. Put the sentences in order to make a conversation.

a. _____ It comes at 11:30.

b. _____ You're welcome.

c. _____ Take the Number 2.

d. __1__ Excuse me, how do I get to the mall?

e. _____ Thank you.

f. _____ What time does it come?

Review

A. Write the correct letter.

a.

b.

c.

d.

e.

f.

g.

h.

i.

j.

k.

l.

1. __d__ apartments

2. _____ bank

3. _____ bus

4. _____ car

5. _____ hospital

6. _____ house

7. _____ pharmacy

8. _____ stop sign

9. _____ supermarket

10. _____ taxi

11. _____ train

12. _____ left turn sign

B. Practice asking and answering the questions with a partner.

1. Where do you live?

2. Where do you buy clothing?

3. Where do you buy shoes?

4. Where do you eat?

Learner Log

I can describe housing.   I can express personal information.
■ Yes   ■ No   ■ Maybe   ■ Yes   ■ No   ■ Maybe

C. Look at the information about Aki and Adriano. Write and practice a conversation.

1. I'm Aki.
   I'm from Japan.
   I live in an apartment.
   I live in New York on Second Street.
   I drive to school.

2. I'm Adriano.
   I'm from Brazil.
   I live in a house.
   I live in New York on East 5th Street.
   I take the subway to school.

Aki: _Hi, Adriano. Where do you live?_ _____

Adriano: _____

Aki: _____

Adriano: _____

Aki: _____

Adriano: _____

D. Write.

1. Aki _____ to school.

2. Adriano _____ to school.

3. They _____ in New York.

E. Read the map.

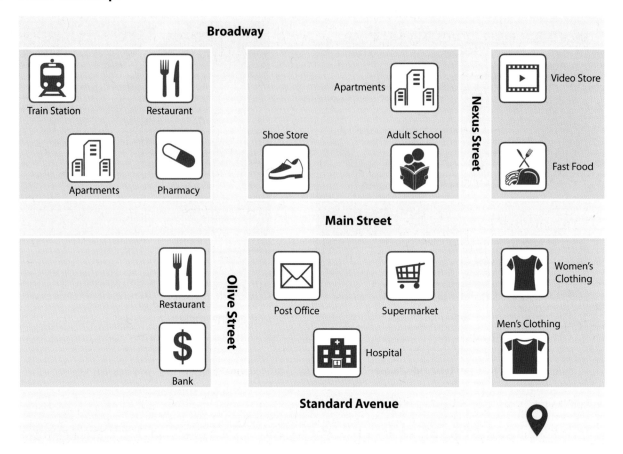

F. Write the place.

Place	Directions
the post office	Turn right on Nexus. Turn left on Main. It's next to the supermarket.
	Go straight. Turn right on Olive Street. It's next to the restaurant.
	Go straight. Turn right on Olive Street. Turn right on Main Street. It's next to the adult school.
	Turn right on Nexus. Turn left on Broadway. Go straight. It's next to the restaurant.

1. **COLLABORATE** Form a team with four or five students. In your team, you need:

Position	Job description	Student name
Student 1: Team Leader	Check that everyone speaks English. Check that everyone participates.	
Student 2: Writer	Write directions.	
Student 3: Artist	Make a map.	
Students 4/5: Spokesperson	Prepare a presentation.	

2. Make a list of types of transportation in your community.

3. Make a map of your community with the school in the middle. Write the names of stores and other places near your school.

4. Write directions from your school to three places in your community.

5. Present your project to the class.

People in the city enjoy a boat ride in the park.

EXPLORER JIMMY CHIN

A Dangerous Commute

"I should have climbed out of the hole for a more secure footing, but I knew the moment would be lost."
—Jimmy Chin

A. PREDICT Look at the picture and answer the questions.

1. Where is Jimmy in the picture?

2. What is his job?

3. How do you think he gets to work?

B. BRAINSTORM In a group, make a list of transportation words.

Type of transportation		Ways to travel	
car	_____	drive	_____
bicycle	_____	walk	_____
_____	_____	_____	_____

C. Read about Jimmy Chin.

Jimmy Chin is from Mankato, Minnesota. He has a very dangerous job: He's a photographer. But is that a dangerous job? Jimmy takes photos of adventurers in some of the world's most interesting places, like Mount Everest. When Jimmy takes photos of climbers, he doesn't take a bus or a train to work; he doesn't walk to work. He climbs to work!

D. COMPARE How does Jimmy get to work? How do you get to school?

Jimmy Chin

Jimmy _____ to work.

Jimmy doesn't _____
to work.

Me

I _____ to work.

I don't _____ to work.

E. APPLY Write about you.

Name	1.
Birthplace	2.
City	3.
Street	4.
Home (apartment / house / mobile home)	5.
Transportation	6.

1. My name is _____.

2. I am from _____.

3. I live in _____.

4. I live on _____.

5. I live in _____.

6. I _____.

F. Tell a group your story. Repeat the sentences in Exercise E.

Healthy Living

Visitors to the Blue Lagoon bathe in
volcanic water and wear mud masks.

UNIT OUTCOMES

Identify body parts

Describe symptoms and illnesses

Identify medications

Describe healthy habits

Identify actions in a waiting room

Look at the photo and answer the questions.

1. What are the people doing? How does it benefit their health?

2. What other ways can you keep healthy?

LESSON **1** **I need a checkup**

GOAL ▪ Identify body parts

A. **Where is the man in the picture? Who is he talking to?**

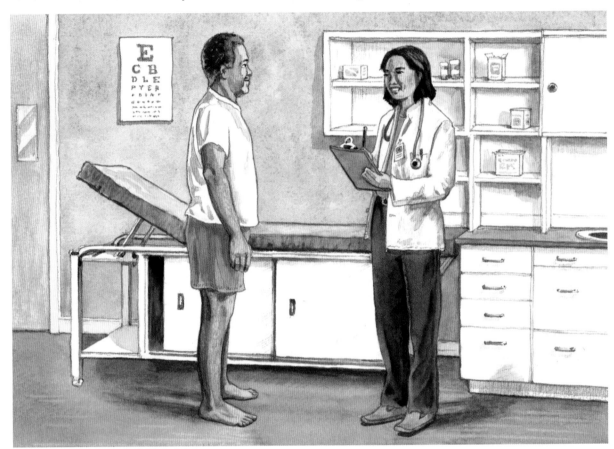

B. **Listen and write.**

CD 2
TR 15

My name is Guillermo. _____ live in Chicago. I _____ 61 years old.

I _____ the doctor once a year for a checkup. I'm very healthy.

C. **Complete the paragraph about yourself. Use Exercise B to help you.**

My name is _____. I am from _____. I _____ years old.

I _____ the doctor _____ a year for a checkup.

D. Read the new words.

head	back	hand	foot
neck	arm	leg	nose

E. Write the new words in the picture.

F. Practice the conversation. Use the words in Exercise D to make new conversations.

Student A: Where's the nose?
Student B: It's here. (points to own nose)

G. Read.

Imperatives			
	Subject	**Verb**	**Example sentence**
Please	~~you~~	read	Please read the chart.
		open	Please open your mouth.
		let me (look)	Please let me look in your ear.
		sit down	Please sit down.
		stand up	Please stand up.

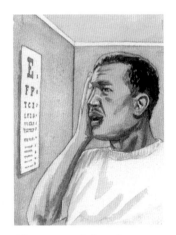

Please read the chart.

Please open your mouth and say "Ah."

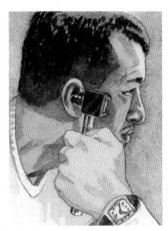

Let me look in your ear.

H. Listen and practice the conversation. Make new conversations.

CD 2
TR 16

Doctor:	<u>Please sit down.</u>
Guillermo:	OK.
Doctor:	<u>Please open your mouth and say, "Ah."</u>
Guillermo:	Ah.

I. APPLY Which body parts does the doctor examine during a checkup? Make a list.

1. _____

2. _____

3. _____

4. _____

LESSON **2** I'm sick!

 A. **Listen and repeat.**

CD 2
TR 17

headache

backache

stomachache

cold and
runny nose

cough and
sore throat

fever

 B. **Listen and point.**

CD 2
TR 18–23

 C. **Listen and check (✓) the correct answer.**

CD 2
TR 24–27

1. **Maritza has** _____

    ☐ a cold.

    ☐ a headache.

    ☐ a fever.

2. **Shan has** _____

    ☐ a backache.

    ☐ a fever.

    ☐ a cold.

3. **John has** _____

    ☐ a runny nose.

    ☐ a fever.

    ☐ a headache.

4. **Anakiya has** _____

    ☐ a fever.

    ☐ a runny nose.

    ☐ a backache.

D. Read about colds and make a list of symptoms.

> **The Common Cold**
> A cold is an illness that usually lasts for up to ten days. There are many symptoms. For example, many people have a runny nose and a sore throat. Others have a low fever. Some people have a cough, too.

1. _____

2. _____

3. _____

4. _____

E. Complete the table.

Symptom	Duration (how long)	Do you see the doctor?	
		Yes ✔	No ✔
runny nose	1 day		
sore throat	1 month		
cough	2 weeks		
low fever	2 days		
high fever	2 days		
headache	3 hours		
stomachache	1 week		

F. Discuss your table in a group.

A cold is an illness that usually lasts up to ten days.

G. Read the charts.

Simple Present with *Be* (Irregular)		
Subject	***Be***	**Example sentence**
I	am	I **am** sick.
You, We, They	are	We **are** sick.
He, She, It	is	He **is** sick.

Simple Present with *Have* (Irregular)		
Subject	***Have***	**Example sentence**
I, You, We, They	have	I **have** a headache.
He, She, It	has	She **has** a runny nose.

H. Write.

1. He _____ (have) a headache.

2. She _____ (be) very sick.

3. I _____ (be) sick.

4. You _____ (have) a cold.

5. Oscar _____ (have) a stomachache.

6. You _____ (be) sick.

I. Practice the conversation. Use the symptoms in Exercise A to make new conversations.

Maritza: How are you?
Shan: I'm sick!
Maritza: What's the matter?
Shan: I have a <u>headache</u>.

LESSON 3 You need aspirin

GOAL ▮ Identify medications

🎧 **A. Read, listen, and write the missing words.**

CD 2
TR 28

	NAME	PROBLEM	PHONE
3:30	Julio Rodriguez		(777) 555-1395
4:00	Huong Pham	fever	(777) 555-3311
4:30	Richard Price		(777) 555-2323
5:00	Mele Ikahihifo	sore throat	(777) 555-5511
5:30	Fred Wharton		(777) 555-9764
6:00	Ayumi Tanaka	backache	(777) 555-8765

Calendar |∨   ⊕ New |∨   Import   Share ∨   🙂 ⚙

◀▶ February 18   View: Day ∨

B. Look at the schedule in Exercise A and write the problems.

__fever__

_____

_____

_____

_____

_____

HAVE	
I, You, We, They	*have*
He, She	*has*

C. Write sentences.

1. Julio has a headache. _____

2. Richard has a _____.

3. Ayumi _____.

D. ANALYZE Look at the medicine bottles. In a group, write the illnesses each medicine is for.

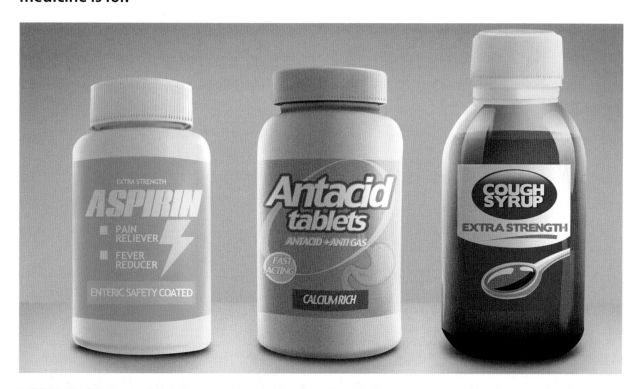

Aspirin	Antacid	Cough Syrup
fever		

E. APPLY Write other types of medicine you take.

_____

_____

_____

_____

_____

F. Read.

Simple Present		
I, You, We, They	need	aspirin
He, She, It	need**s**	antacid

G. Write sentences. Use *need*.

1. Julio has a headache. _He needs aspirin._____

2. Huong has a fever. _He_____.

3. Richard has a stomachache. _He_____.

4. Mele has a sore throat and cough. _She_____.

5. Fred has a cold. _He_____.

6. Ayumi and Sue have backaches. _They_____.

7. Tami and I have stomachaches. _We_____.

8. Shiuli and Sang have sore throats. _They_____.

H. What types of medicine do you have at home? Write.

_____

_____

_____

_____

_____

_____

_____

I. Speak to family members. What home remedies do you or your family use? Tell them to the class.

LESSON ④ Exercise every day!

GOAL ▦ Describe healthy habits

A. INTERPRET Read and listen.

MAIN STREET HEALTH CENTER

We are happy you are a patient of Dr. Ramsey. Our goal is to help you stay healthy. Follow these suggestions and you will be healthier.

DO'S

Sleep:
Sleep 7-8 hours a night.

Exercise:
Walk, run, or do some other form of exercise 30 minutes a day.

Eat:
Eat three good meals a day.

See the Doctor:
See the doctor once a year for a checkup,

DONT'S

Don't smoke!

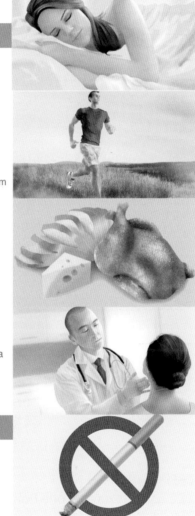

B. Practice with a partner.

Dr. Ramsey: How many hours do you sleep a night?
Hasna: I sleep four hours a night.
Dr. Ramsey: That is not healthy. You need to sleep seven to eight hours.

C. Listen and read Huong's story. Why is Huong healthy?

CD 2
TR 30

> I'm healthy. I exercise one hour every day. I eat breakfast, lunch, and dinner. I don't eat a lot of candy. I don't smoke. I sleep seven hours every night.

D. What does Huong do? Fill in the table.

What does Huong do?	What doesn't Huong do?
exercise	

E. Read the charts.

Simple Present		
Subject	**Verb**	**Example sentence**
I, You, We, They	eat	I **eat** three meals a day.
He, She, It	sleeps	She **sleeps** seven hours a night.

Negative Simple Present			
Subject	**Verb**		**Example sentence**
I, You, We, They	**don't**	eat	We **don't eat** three meals a day.
He, She, It	**doesn't**	sleep	He **doesn't sleep** seven hours a day.

F. Write about Huong.

1. Huong _____exercises_____ (exercise) one hour every day.

2. Huong _____ (sleep) seven hours every night.

3. Huong _____ (eat) breakfast, lunch, and dinner.

4. Huong _____ (smoke).

5. Huong _____ (eat) a lot of candy.

G. Look at the pictures and read the information in the table.

Julia

Hasna

Dalmar

Name	Julia	Hasna	Dalmar
Sleep	8 hours	5 hours	8 hours
Meals	breakfast, lunch, dinner	lunch, dinner	breakfast, lunch, dinner
Exercise	30 minutes a day	0 minutes a day	20 minutes a day
Checkup	once a year	once a year	0 times a year
Smoke	no	no	yes

H. Write.

1. Julia and Hasna ___*don't smoke*___ (smoke).

2. Hasna _____ (eat) breakfast.

3. Dalmar and Julia _____ (sleep) eight hours every day.

4. Hasna _____ (exercise).

5. Julia and Hasna _____ (see) the doctor for a checkup.

6. Dalmar _____ (see) the doctor for a checkup.

I. Write.

Your name: _____   Exercise: _____

Sleep: _____   Checkup: _____

Meals: _____   Smoke: _____

GOAL ▮ Identify actions in a waiting room

A. Use the words in the box to talk about the picture.

| talk | wait | read | answer | sleep |

B. Listen to the conversation and put the actions in order. Write 1–5.

CD 2
TR 31

_____ talk (are talking)

___1___ wait (are waiting)

_____ read (is reading)

_____ answer (am answering)

_____ sleep (is sleeping)

C. Read the chart.

Present Continuous (right now)			
Subject	*Be*	**Base +** *ing*	**Example sentence**
I	am	talking	I **am talking.**
He, She, It	is	sleeping	He **is sleeping.**
We, You, They	are	waiting	They **are waiting.**

D. Listen and repeat.

CD 2
TR 32

talking
waiting
reading
sleeping

E. Look at the picture in Exercise A. Write.

1. The receptionist ___is___ _____answering_____ (answer) the phone now.

2. The man in the white shirt _____ _____ (sleep) in the chair now.

3. The people _____ _____ (wait) for the doctor now.

4. The women _____ _____ (talk) about their children now.

5. Guillermo _____ _____ (read) a magazine now.

F. With a partner, ask and answer the questions about the picture in Exercise A.

What is the receptionist doing now?
What is the man in the white shirt doing now?
What are the people doing now?
What are the women doing now?
What is Guillermo doing now?

G. Look at the picture.

H. Talk about the picture with a partner.

I. Imagine you are in a waiting room. Write sentences.

1. _____

2. _____

3. _____

4. _____

▶ **I've got a lot of stress**

Before You Watch

A. Look at the picture and answer the questions.

1. What is wrong with Mr. Sanchez?

2. Who is the man in the white coat?

While You Watch

B. ▶ **Watch the video and complete the dialog. Use the words in the box.**

do	don't	ear	normal	~~mouth~~	sleep

Doctor: Your heart rate is normal. Can you open your (1) _____ *mouth* _____ and go "Ah."

Victor: Ah.

Doctor: Good. Now let me look inside your (2) _____.

Victor: What (3) _____ you see?

Doctor: Everything looks fine. All your vital signs are (4) _____. Tell me, what brings you in today?

Victor: Well, I'm very tired all the time. I (5) _____ have any energy.

Doctor: Do you get enough (6) _____?

Check Your Understanding

C. Put the sentences in order to make a conversation.

a. _____ **Patient:** About five hours a night.

b. __1__ **Doctor:** How are you feeling?

c. _____ **Patient:** I think you're right. Thanks for the advice, doctor.

d. _____ **Doctor:** How much sleep do you get?

e. _____ **Patient:** Not well. I'm tired all the time.

f. _____ **Doctor:** That's not enough. You should get at least seven hours a night.

Review

A. Write the body parts.

head	stomach	hand	foot
neck	arm	leg	nose

B. Write the symptom or illness.

stomach _____stomachache_____

head _____

back _____

throat _____

nose _____

C. **Complete the sentences with the present continuous.**

1. The receptionist _____ _____ (talk) on the phone.

2. The patient _____ _____ (sleep).

3. The people _____ _____ (wait) for the doctor.

4. The women _____ _____ (ask) about their children.

5. Hector _____ _____ (read) a magazine.

D. **Write the medicines.**

1. Richard has a headache. What does he need?

   Medicine: _____

2. Orlando has a stomachache. What does he need?

   Medicine: _____

3. Hue has a fever. What does she need?

   Medicine: _____

4. Chan has a sore throat. What does he need?

   Medicine: _____

E. **Read and write in the chart.**

Jeremiah is not very healthy. He smokes ten cigarettes a day. He doesn't exercise. He eats one meal a day. He doesn't sleep eight hours a night. He doesn't drink water. He sees the doctor once a year.

What does Jeremiah do?	What doesn't Jeremiah do?

F. **Complete the sentences with the simple present.**

1. She _____ (have) a headache.

2. They _____ (need) medicine.

3. We _____ (be) sick.

4. I _____ (be) healthy.

5. You _____ (exercise) every day.

6. Mario and Maria _____ (visit) the doctor.

7. He _____ (sleep) eight hours a day.

8. Alfonso _____ (smoke) cigarettes.

G. **Complete the sentences with the negative simple present.**

1. He _____ (smoke) every day.

2. They _____ (eat) breakfast.

3. We _____ (need) medicine.

4. They _____ (exercise).

5. Nga _____ (have) a headache.

6. She _____ (visit) the doctor.

7. I _____ (want) lunch.

8. You _____ (exercise).

TEAM PROJECT ✔ At the doctor's office

1. **COLLABORATE** Form a team with four or five students. In your team, you need:

Position	Job description	Student name
Student 1: Team Leader	Check that everyone speaks English. Check that everyone participates.	
Student 2: Writer	Write conversations to act out.	
Student 3: Artist	Make an appointment book page.	
Students 4/5: Spokespeople	Prepare a presentation.	

2. Prepare your roles.

   Who is the doctor? _____

   Who is Patient 1? _____

   Who is Patient 2? _____

   Who is the receptionist? _____

3. Make an appointment book page.

   What is Patient 1's name?

   When is the appointment?

   What is the problem?

   Write a conversation between the receptionist and Patient 1.

   Write a conversation between the doctor and Patient 1.

4. Write conversations for Patient 2.

5. Present your conversations and appointment book page to the class.

EXPLORER DIANA NYAD

The 100-Mile Swim

"You have to believe you are going across. There are no ifs. You are making it."
—Diana Nyad

A. PREDICT Look at the picture and circle the answers you think are correct.

1. **Where is Diana Nyad?**

   a. in a pool   b. in a lake   c. in the ocean   d. in a river

2. **What do you think the article is about?**

   a. the ocean   b. swimming   c. sports   d. healthy foods

B. In a group, take turns talking about your favorite sport.

C. Read about Diana Nyad.

It's 2012; Diana Nyad wants to swim from Havana, Cuba to Florida in the United States. The distance between the two countries is over 100 miles, and there are sharks and jellyfish in the water! But, Diana is a professional swimmer. For a long time, she exercises, eats healthy food, and trains to get ready. It's now 2013, and on her fifth attempt, Diana successfully makes it all the way—110.86 miles—from Cuba to the United States.

D. Check your answers in Exercise A. Ask and answer with a partner.

1. Where is Diana Nyad?

2. What is the story about?

E. Answer the questions about the article and complete the table.

1. What does Diana do to get ready?

   She _____, _____ healthy foods, and

   _____.

2. What dangers are in the water?

   _____ and _____ are in the water.

Everyday activities	Dangers in the water
_____	_____
_____	_____
_____	

F. CREATE What healthy things do you do every day? Make a list.

_____

_____

_____

_____

_____

Work

Fishermen surrounded by seagulls fish for anchovies.

UNIT OUTCOMES

- Identify occupations
- Give information about work
- Identify job duties
- Read evaluations
- Follow directions

Look at the photo and answer the questions.

1. What job do you think the men on the boat have?

2. What do you think their job duties are?

LESSON **1** Do you work?

GOAL ■ Identify occupations

A. PREDICT Look at the picture. What are the people talking about?

🎧 **B. Listen and read.**

CD 2
TR 33

> My name is Emilio. I live in Dallas, Texas. I have a new job. I'm a cashier at Ultra Supermarket on Broadway! This is a picture of my class.

C. Write. What does Emilio do?

He's a student; he's also a _____.

162   Unit 7

D. Listen and repeat the words. What do these people do?

Emilio
cashier

Hue
doctor

Chan
bus driver

Carolina
student

Davit
salesperson

Pete
teacher

E. Practice the conversation with a partner. Use the words in Exercise D.

Student A: What does <u>Emilio</u> do?
Student B: He's a <u>cashier</u>.

F. Write sentences about the people in Exercise D.

1. Emilio is a cashier. _____

2. Hue _____.

3. _____

4. _____

5. _____

6. _____

Lesson 1   163

G. CLASSIFY Write the jobs in the table.

cook	custodian	mail carrier	manager	nurse

School	Restaurant	Clothing store	Community	Doctor's office
teacher	cashier	salesperson	bus driver	doctor

H. Practice the conversation. Use the information in Exercise G to make new conversations.

Student A: Where does <u>a teacher</u> work?
Student B: A teacher works in a <u>school</u>.

SIMPLE PRESENT	
I work.	I don't work.
He works.	He doesn't work.
She works.	She doesn't work.

I. Read the conversation.

Student A: Do you work?
Student B: Yes, I work. I'm a <u>cashier</u>. How about you? Do you work?
Student A: No, I don't work. I'm a <u>student</u>.

J. Practice the conversation in Exercise I with four classmates and complete the table.

Name	Occupation

K. What do your friends and family do? Make a list.

GOAL   Give information about work

A. PREDICT   Write the jobs from the box. Then, listen to check your answers.

CD 2
TR 35

manager	receptionist	custodian

1.

Name: Isabel
Title: _____
Company: Johnson Company
Supervisor: Martin
Hours: 9 a.m. to 6 p.m.
Break: 12 p.m. to 1 p.m.
Days: Monday to Friday

2.

Name: Cory
Title: _____
Company: Freedman's Foods
Supervisor: Amelia
Hours: 2 p.m. to 10 p.m.
Break: 6 p.m. to 7 p.m.
Days: Wednesday to Sunday

3.

Name: Fred
Title: _____
Company: America Bank
Supervisor: Mary
Hours: 10 p.m. to 7 a.m.
Break: 1 a.m. to 2 a.m.
Days: Sunday to Friday

B.   **Listen and write the names of the people from Exercise A.**

CD 2
TR 36

1. _____   2. _____   3. _____

C. Read.

Question word	Type of answer	Example sentence with *be*	Example sentence with *do*
What	Asking for information	What **is your** name? What **is his** name?	What **do you** do? What **does** he do?
Where	Asking about a place or position	Where **is your** office? Where **is her** office?	Where **do you** work? Where **does she** work?
When	Asking about time	When **is your** break? When **is his** break?	When **do you** work? When **does he** work?
Who	Asking about a person	Who **is your** supervisor? Who **is her** supervisor?	Who **do you** like? Who **does she** like?

D. Match the questions and answers about Cory.

1. What do you do?
2. Where do you work?
3. Who is your supervisor?
4. When do you work?
5. When is your break?

a. I work at Freedman's Foods.

b. It's from 6:00 p.m. to 7:00 p.m.

c. I work Wednesday through Sunday.

d. I'm a manager.

e. Amelia.

E. With a partner, ask and answer the questions in Exercise D. Take turns being Isabel, Cory, and Fred from Exercise A.

F. Read.

My name is Ben. I'm a nurse. I work at a hospital from 7:00 a.m. to 7:00 p.m. I work Monday through Thursday. I help the doctors and talk to patients. My supervisor is Dr. O'Malley.

G. Answer the questions.

1. What does Ben do? He's a _____.

2. When does he start work? He starts work at _____.

3. Where does he work? He works at _____.

4. Who is Ben's supervisor? His supervisor is _____.

H. Listen. Complete the chart about Tan, Maria, and Alfredo.

CD 2
TR 37–39

	What	When	Where
Tan	custodian		
Maria	manager		
Alfredo	nurse		

I. Practice the conversation. Use the information in Exercise H to make new conversations. Ask and answer questions about Tan, Maria, and Alfredo.

Student A: *What* does Tan do?
Student B: He's a custodian.

J. APPLY Answer the questions.

1. What do you do? _____

2. Where do you work or go to school? _____

3. Who is your supervisor or teacher? _____

4. When do you work or go to school? _____

LESSON **3** What do you do?

GOAL ▓ Identify job duties

A. Listen and write.

CD 2
TR 40

| answer phones | talk to customers | send memos | change light bulbs |

1. _____

2. _____

3. _____

4. _____

B. What do they do? Listen and write.

CD 2
TR 41

| supervises employees | helps doctors | makes change |
| answers phones | talks to customers | ~~sends memos~~ | mops floors |

Occupation	Job description
1. administrative assistant	sends memos
2. custodian	
3. receptionist	
4. salesperson	
5. cashier	
6. manager	
7. nurse	

C. Read.

A receptionist schedules meetings.

Sometimes, workers take breaks.

D. APPLY Complete the chart.

	mops	answers phones	talks to customers	sends memos	takes breaks	schedules meetings
salesperson		x	x		x	
administrative assistant						
receptionist						
custodian						

YES/NO QUESTIONS

Does he clean?

Does she schedule meetings?

Does he talk to customers?

E. Answer the questions. Check (✓) *Yes* or *No*. Practice with a partner.

	Yes	No
1. Does a salesperson supervise employees?	_____	✓
2. Does an administrative assistant take breaks?	_____	_____
3. Does a custodian talk to customers?	_____	_____
4. Does a receptionist talk to customers?	_____	_____
5. Does a salesperson mop the floors?	_____	_____

F.   Read.

Can			
Subject	**Can**	**Verb (base)**	**Example sentence**
I, You, He, She, It, We, They	can	send	I can send memos.
		change	He can change a light bulb.

Can't			
Subject	**Can't**	**Verb (base)**	**Example sentence**
I, You, He, She, It, We, They	can't	send	I can't send memos.
		change	He can't change a light bulb.

G.   Complete the sentences with *can* + the verb.

1. He _____ can file _____ (file) papers.

2. They _____ (send) memos.

3. I _____ (mop) the floor.

4. You _____ (answer) phones.

H.   Complete the sentences with *can't* + the verb.

1. We _____ can't take _____ (take) breaks.

2. They _____ (type).

3. I _____ (talk) to customers.

4. She _____ (file).

I.   APPLY   Write what you *can* and *can't* do. Use words from this lesson.

1. I can _____ .   1. I can't _____ .

2. _____ .   2. _____ .

GOAL ▨ Read evaluations

A. Read.

Name: Emilio Sanchez		
Work Evaluation		
	Yes	No
1. Helps customers	✓	
2. Comes to work on time	✓	
3. Speaks English well	✓	
4. Follows directions well	✓	
Manager Signature: Calvin Carter		

B. ANALYZE What does a good student do? Circle.

sends memos	does homework	practices English
(listens)	talks to customers	takes lunch breaks
cleans the office	comes to school on time	follows directions
schedules meetings	reads in class	writes in class

C. COLLABORATE In groups, add more ideas.

_____

_____

_____

_____

_____

_____

D. Read.

Simple Present: *Be*		
Subject	***Be***	**Example sentence**
I	am	I **am** friendly.
He, She, It	is	She **is** helpful.
We, You, They	are	They **are** careful.

Simple Present: *Be* (negative)		
Subject	***Be* (Negative)**	**Example sentence**
I	am not	I **am not** cheerful.
He, She, It	is not	She **is not** helpful.
We, You, They	are not	They **are not** friendly.

E. Write the correct form of the verb *Be*.

1. Emilio _____ friendly with the customers.

2. Carolina _____ not cheerful.

3. We _____ helpful.

4. They _____ not careful.

F. Listen and check.

Name: Alice Eriksson		
Work Evaluation		
	Yes	**No**
1. Is careful		
2. Is friendly		
3. Is helpful		
4. Is cheerful		
Manager Signature: Jan Brown		

G. Read.

Davit Deluse is a salesperson. He works Monday through Friday. He always helps customers, and he is always friendly. Sometimes he is not careful with clothing, and sometimes he doesn't come to work on time.

H. EVALUATE Read about Davit again in Exercise G and complete the evaluation.

Name: Davit Deluse		
Work Evaluation		
	Yes	No
1. Helps customers		
2. Comes to work on time		
3. Is friendly		
4. Is careful		
Manager Signature: Calvin Carter		

I. APPLY Complete an evaluation for yourself at school.

School Evaluation		
	Yes	No
1. I come to school on time.		
2. I follow directions.		
3. I do my homework.		
4. I am cheerful and friendly.		

LESSON **5** Please send the memo

GOAL ▦ Follow directions

🎧 **A.** **Listen and point.**

CD 2
TR 43

1. Don't smoke.

2. Wash your hands.

3. Don't eat in the office.

Fred, please
answer the phones.

Fred, please
send the memos.

Fred, please
schedule a meeting.

4. Fred, please answer
   the phones.

5. Fred, please send
   the memos.

6. Fred, please schedule
   a meeting.

B. **Read the signs and notes in Exercise A. Circle *Yes* or *No*.**

1. Smoke.	Yes	(No)
2. Wash hands.	Yes	No
3. Eat.	Yes	No
4. Answer the phones.	Yes	No
5. Send the memos.	Yes	No
6. Schedule a meeting.	Yes	No

C. Read.

Affirmative Commands			
	Verb		**Example sentence**
You	wash	your hands	Wash your hands.
	answer	the phones	Answer the phones.
	send	the memos	Send the memos.

Negative Commands			
	Verb		**Example sentence**
You	don't	smoke	Don't smoke.
		eat	Don't eat.
		send	the memos	Don't send the memos.

D. Complete the sentences.

1. Wash your hands _____.

2. Send _____.

3. Answer _____.

4. Don't _____.

E. Read and practice the conversations. Use the commands in Exercise C.

Manager: How are you, Isabel?
Isabel: I'm fine, thank you.
Manager: Please send the memos.
Isabel: Yes, of course.

Manager: How are you, Isabel?
Isabel: I'm fine, thank you.
Manager: Please don't eat in the office.
Isabel: No, of course not.

F. INTERPRET Read.

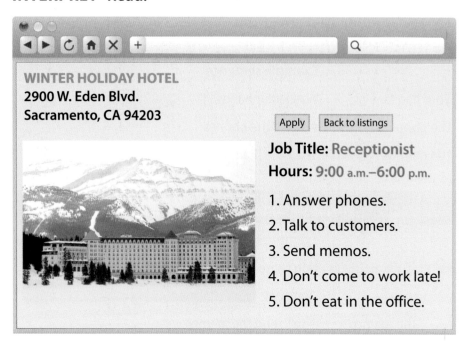

G. Look at the job description in Exercise F. Write the commands.

Do's	Don'ts
Answer phones.	

H. CREATE In groups, write classroom _do's_ and _don'ts_.

Classroom Do's	Classroom Don'ts
Listen.	

Before You Watch

A. Look at the picture and answer the questions.

1. What job does Hector have?

2. What is he doing?

While You Watch

B. Watch the video and complete the dialog. Use the words in the box.

cleans	custodian	mops	~~receptionist~~	takes

Hector: Why not? What does a (1) _____ *receptionist* _____ do?

Mrs. Sanchez: A receptionist answers phones and (2) _____ messages.

Hector: I don't think so. What about a custodian? What does a (3) _____ do?

Mr. Sanchez: A custodian mops the floor and (4) _____ windows.

Hector: (5) _____ the floor?

Check Your Understanding

C. Show the correct order of the events by writing a number next to each sentence.

a. _____   Hector reads an ad for a custodian.

b. _____   Hector reads ads for sales clerks.

c. __1__   Mrs. Sanchez tells Hector what a receptionist does.

d. _____   Mr. Sanchez says what a custodian does.

e. _____   Hector calls Mateo on his cell phone.

A. Write the name of the job.

1.

_____

2.

_____

3.

_____

4.

_____

5.

_____

6.

_____

7.

_____

8.

_____

B. Point to a picture in Exercise A. Ask a partner about the job.

Student A: What does <u>he</u> do?

Student B: He's a <u>custodian</u>.

Learner Log

I can give information about work.   I can identify job duties.
■ Yes ■ No ■ Maybe   ■ Yes ■ No ■ Maybe

C. Match the job with the duty. Draw a line.

1.

                   a. sends memos

2.

                   b. makes change

3.

                   c. changes light bulbs

4.

                   d. talks to customers

D. Write *when, where, what,* or *who*. Responses can be used more than once.

1. _____ does the store open? The store opens at 10:00 a.m.

2. _____ do you take a break? I take a break in the cafeteria.

3. _____ do you work? I work in Sacramento.

4. _____ is your manager? His name is Martin.

5. _____ does she do? She's a nurse.

E. Identify the signs.

1. _____

2. _____

3. _____

F. COMPARE What can you do? What can your partner do? Complete the chart.

EXAMPLES: I can speak English well.

I can follow directions.

I can schedule meetings.

I can

We can

My partner can

TEAM PROJECT ✓ Start a company

1. **COLLABORATE** Form a team with four or five students. In your team, you need:

Position	Job description	Student name
Student 1: Team Leader	Check that everyone speaks English. Check that everyone participates.	
Student 2: Writer	Write job descriptions.	
Student 3: Artist	Make a cover page with the name of your company and a logo.	
Students 4/5: Spokespeople	Prepare a presentation.	

2. What is the name of your company?
   What is your company logo? Make a cover page.

3. What are the jobs in the company?

4. Write three job descriptions for jobs in your company.

5. Present your company to the class.

Offices for new companies sometimes look different from normal offices.

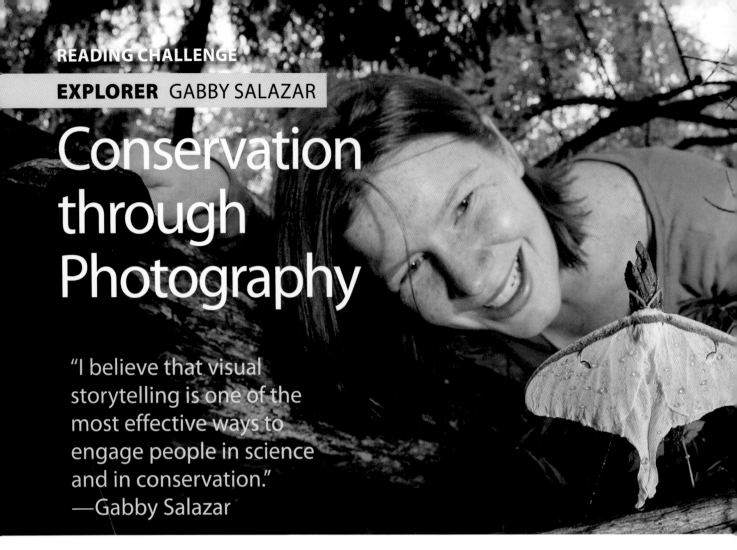

Conservation through Photography

"I believe that visual storytelling is one of the most effective ways to engage people in science and in conservation."
—Gabby Salazar

A. PREDICT Look at the picture and answer the questions.

1. Where is Gabby?

2. What do you think her job is?

3. What are her job duties?

B. SURVEY Ask three classmates what they do. Complete the sentences.

1. _____Ana_____ is a _____cook_____. He/She (circled) makes food _____.

2. _____ is a _____. He/She _____.

3. _____ is a _____. He/She _____.

4. _____ is a _____. He/She _____.

C. Read about Gabby Salazar.

Gabby Salazar is a nature photographer from North Carolina. She likes to take photos of rare and interesting plants, animals, and insects. She can take good photos, so good that she wins awards and her photos appear in magazines! Gabby can also speak well to people. With her photos, Gabby teaches people how to care for the natural world.

D. What two things can Gabby do? Write one thing you can do.

1. Gabby can _____.

2. Gabby can _____.

3. I can _____.

E. BRAINSTORM What can people take pictures of? Complete the chart.

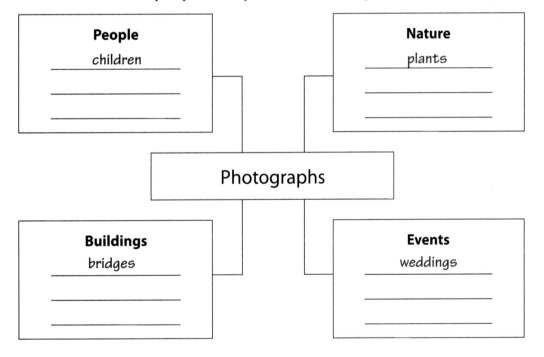

People
children
_____
_____
_____

Nature
plants
_____
_____
_____

Photographs

Buildings
bridges
_____
_____
_____

Events
weddings
_____
_____
_____

F. APPLY What do you take pictures of? Discuss in a group.

EXAMPLE: I take pictures of my children to show to my friends.

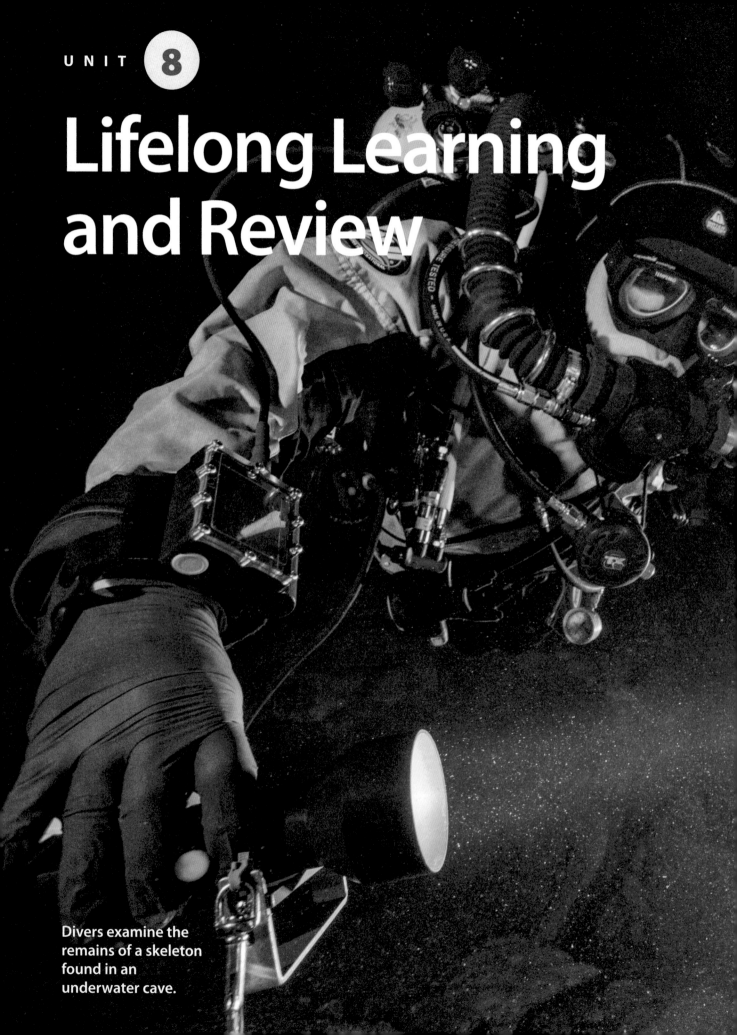

Lifelong Learning and Review

Divers examine the remains of a skeleton found in an underwater cave.

UNIT OUTCOMES

☐ Organize study materials

☐ Make purchases

☐ Give and follow directions

☐ Make goals

☐ Develop a study schedule

Look at the photo and answer the questions.

1. What job do the people have?

2. What can they learn from what they have found?

LESSON ❶ Let's get organized!

GOAL ▬ Organize study materials

🎧 A. Listen and repeat.
CD 2
TR 44

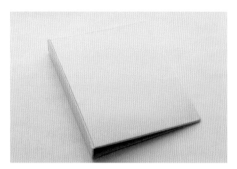

binder

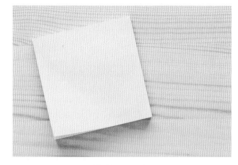

sticky notes

dividers

paper clips

sheets of lined paper

highlighter pen

B. COLLABORATE In a group, write more items you use to organize your study materials.

_____   _____

_____   _____

_____   _____

C. Listen and choose the correct answer.

1. What size binder do they need?

☐ 1 inch

☐ 1 ½ inches

☐ 3 inches

2. How many dividers do they need?

☐ one divider

☐ three dividers

☐ five dividers

3. How many sheets of lined paper do they need?

☐ 50 sheets

☐ 100 sheets

☐ 200 sheets

D. Look through units 1–7. For your binder, write the page numbers and two words for each section.

Section	Reference pages	Example vocabulary
Basic Communication (Pre-Unit, Unit 1, and Unit 2)	2–59	
Consumer Economics (Unit 3 and Unit 4)		
Community Resources (Unit 5)		
Health (Unit 6)		
Occupational Knowledge (Unit 7)		

E. **Interview and write about your partner. Report to a group.**

1. What's your name? _____

2. Where do you live? _____

3. What is your phone number? _____

4. What is your date of birth? _____

5. Are you married? _____

6. Where are you from? _____

F. **CREATE** **Make a personal profile like the one below on a separate piece of paper. Use it as the first page of your binder.**

PERSONAL PROFILE
School: _____
Teacher: _____
First Name: _____
Middle Name: _____
Last Name: _____
Address: _____
City: _____
State: _____
Zip: _____
Country: _____
Marital Status (circle):   Single   Married   Divorced

LESSON ② I need paper

GOAL ▨ Make purchases

A. Read the advertisement.

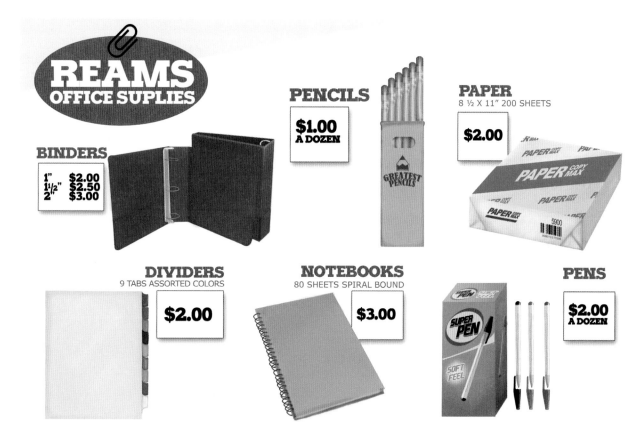

IS / ARE

How much **is** the paper?

How much **are** the notebooks?

B. Listen to the conversation about the ad and practice the conversation.

CD 2
TR 46

Customer:	Excuse me, how much are the dividers?
Salesperson:	They are $2.00 for a set of nine.
Customer:	Thanks. I need one set, please.

C. Listen and repeat.

I need …
    a box of pencils.
    a two-inch binder.
    a set of five colored dividers.
    a package of paper.
    a box of ballpoint pens.
    a notebook.

> **INCHES**
> a two-inch binder = a 2″ binder

D. Look at the ad in Exercise A and write three more items you want. Write the total.

E. Practice the conversation. Use the information in Exercise A to make new conversations.

Salesperson:	What do you need?
Customer:	I need a <u>two-inch binder.</u>
Salesperson:	They are over here.
Customer:	How much are they?
Salesperson:	They are <u>$3.00</u> each.

F. **APPLY** Visit an office supply store in person or online and check prices.

G. In a group, make a list of food you can buy in a supermarket.

Food	Price

H. In a group, make a list of clothing you can buy in a clothing store.

Clothing	Price

I. Look at Exercise E. Write and practice new conversations about your lists in exercises G and H.

J. **CREATE** Look back at units 3 and 4. Prepare a section about *Consumer Economics* in your binder.

Clothing Vocabulary

_____   _____

_____   _____

_____   _____

Food Vocabulary

_____   _____

_____   _____

_____   _____

Questions and Sentences

_____

_____

_____

_____

_____

_____

LESSON ③ Where's the office supply store?

GOAL ▊ Give and follow directions

A. PREDICT Look at the picture. What is happening?

🎧 **B. Listen to the conversation. Write.**

CD 2
TR 48

Woman:	Excuse me, where is Reams Office Supplies?
Man:	It's on First Street.
Woman:	Where's First Street?
Man:	Go straight on this street. Turn _____ on Main Street and _____ on First. It's _____ the electronics store.
Woman:	Thanks.

C. **INTERPRET** Read.

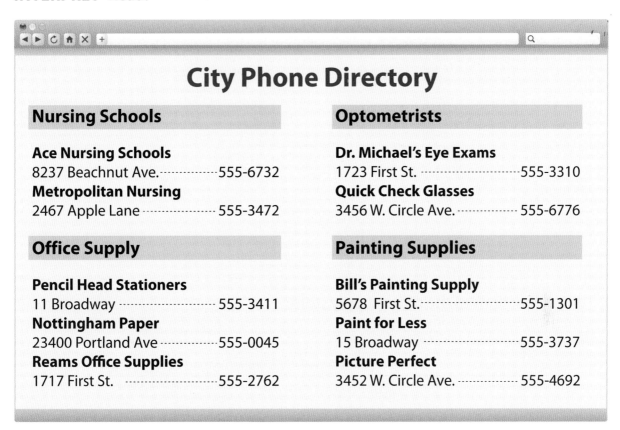

City Phone Directory

Nursing Schools

Ace Nursing Schools
8237 Beachnut Ave. ··············555-6732
Metropolitan Nursing
2467 Apple Lane ·············· 555-3472

Office Supply

Pencil Head Stationers
11 Broadway ···················· 555-3411
Nottingham Paper
23400 Portland Ave ············555-0045
Reams Office Supplies
1717 First St. ···················555-2762

Optometrists

Dr. Michael's Eye Exams
1723 First St. ····················555-3310
Quick Check Glasses
3456 W. Circle Ave. ·············· 555-6776

Painting Supplies

Bill's Painting Supply
5678 First St. ····················555-1301
Paint for Less
15 Broadway ···················· 555-3737
Picture Perfect
3452 W. Circle Ave. ·············· 555-4692

D. Read the conversation.

Man: Excuse me, where is <u>Reams Office Supplies</u>?
Woman: It's on <u>First Street</u>.
Man: What's the address?
Woman: It's <u>1717 First Street</u>.
Man: Thanks.

E. Practice the conversation in Exercise D. Use the information in Exercise C to make new conversations.

F. CREATE Draw a map from your school to an office supply store in your community.

PREPOSITIONS

It's *next to* the bank.

It's *between* the bank and the store.

It's *on* the corner.

G. Write directions to the office supply store.

_____

_____

_____

_____

H. Look back at Unit 5. Prepare a section about *Community* in your binder.

Important Vocabulary

_____   _____

_____   _____

_____   _____

Questions and Sentences

_____

_____

_____

_____

_____

LESSON (4) Sleep eight hours a night

GOAL ▧ Make goals

A. Read Carina's goals.

> ### My Goals
>
> ☑ Sleep eight hours a night.
> ☐ Go to school every day.
> ☐ Exercise one hour a day.
> ☑ Eat three good meals a day.
> ☐ Study English at home one hour a day.
> ☑ Read an article in English online.
> ☐ Watch the news in English online.

B. Listen and check Liang's three goals.

CD 2
TR 49

☐ Sleep eight hours a night.

☐ Go to school every day.

☐ Exercise one hour a day.

☐ Eat three good meals a day.

☐ Study English at home one hour a day.

☐ Read an article in English online.

☐ Watch the news in English online.

C. Talk about Carina's and Liang's goals.

EXAMPLE: Liang's goal is to sleep eight hours a night.

Exercising one hour a day
is a good health habit.

D. INTERPRET Study the two graphs about Liang's class.

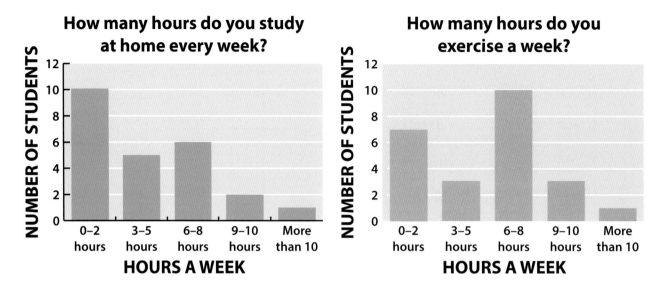

E. SURVEY Take a class poll. Ask, "How many hours do you study at home every week?" Create a bar graph with the information.

How many hours do you study at home every week?

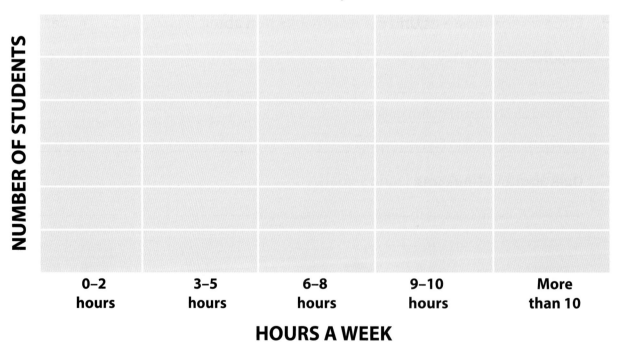

F. **Interview a partner. Write his or her answers.**

1. How many hours do you exercise every week? _____

2. How many hours do you sleep every night? _____

3. How many hours do you study every day? _____

4. How many meals do you eat every day? _____

5. How many days do you go to school a week? _____

G. **APPLY** **Write your goals.**

_____

_____

_____

_____

_____

_____

H. **CREATE** **Look back at Unit 6. Prepare a section about *Health* in your binder.**

Important Vocabulary

_____   _____

_____   _____

_____   _____

Questions and Sentences

_____

_____

_____

_____

_____

_____

LESSON **5** When can I study?

GOAL ▨ Develop a study schedule

🎧 **A. Listen and point to the student and the teacher.**
CD 2
TR 50

B. CLASSIFY Look at the teacher and student duties. Complete the table.

| help students | study at home | come to class on time |
| study new words | prepare lessons | do homework |

Student duties	Teacher duties
	help students

C. Add more duties to the table in Exercise B.

198   Unit 8

D. INTERPRET Read and talk about the schedule. When does Liang work? When does Liang study?

LIANG'S SCHEDULE

	Sunday	Monday	Tuesday	Wednesday	Thursday	Friday	Saturday
6:00 a.m.	Breakfast	Breakfast	Breakfast	Breakfast	Breakfast	Breakfast	Breakfast
9:00 a.m.		School	School	School	School	Study	Study
11:00 a.m.	Lunch	Lunch	Lunch	Lunch	Lunch	Lunch	Lunch
1:00 p.m.		Study	Study	Study	Study	Study	Study
3:00 p.m.							
5:00 p.m.		Work	Work	Work	Work	Work	
7:00 p.m.	Dinner	Dinner	Dinner	Dinner	Dinner	Dinner	Dinner
9:00 p.m.							

E. Answer the questions.

1. When do you study at school? _____

2. When do you study at home? _____

3. When do you work? _____

4. When do you eat breakfast, lunch, and dinner? _____, _____, _____

F. CREATE Complete your schedule.

MY SCHEDULE

	Sunday	Monday	Tuesday	Wednesday	Thursday	Friday	Saturday

G. **Read and talk about Liang's evaluation.**

> **Name:** Liang Ochoa
>
> Studies at home   (Yes)   No
>
> Comes to class on time   Yes   (No)
>
> Speaks English in class   Yes   (No)
>
> Is organized   (Yes)   No
>
> Teacher's signature: _Jennifer Douglas_

H. **Ask questions about Liang.**

EXAMPLE: Does Liang study at home?

I. **EVALUATE** **Complete an evaluation about yourself. Ask your teacher to sign it.**

> Name: _____
>
> Studies at home   Yes   No
>
> Comes to class on time   Yes   No
>
> Speaks English in class   Yes   No
>
> Is organized   Yes   No
>
> Teacher's signature: _____

J. **Look back at Unit 7. Prepare a section about *Occupational Knowledge* in your binder.**

Important Vocabulary

_____   _____

_____   _____

_____   _____

Questions and Sentences

_____

_____

_____

LIFESKILLS ▶ It's easy to get organized

Before You Watch

A. Look at the picture and answer the questions.

1. Where are Hector and Mateo?

2. What's wrong with Mateo?

While You Watch

B. Watch the video and complete the dialog. Use the words in the box.

dividers	have	need	notebook	~~organized~~	What

Hector: Look, Mateo. It's easy to get (1) _____organized_____. You just put everything in a binder with dividers.

Mateo: How many (2) _____ do I need?

Hector: How many classes do you (3) _____?

Mateo: Five—I have five classes.

Hector: Then you (4) _____ five dividers, one for each class. Here, I'll give you some of my dividers.

Mateo: (5) _____ else do you think I need?

Hector: You need pencils, pens, a package of paper, and a (6) _____.

Check Your Understanding

C. Show the correct order of the events by writing a number next to each sentence.

a. _____ Mateo can't find his vocabulary list.

b. _____ Hector tells Mateo what he needs to get organized.

c. _____ Hector gives Mateo some dividers for his notebook.

d. __1__ Mrs. Smith gives the class an extra reading.

e. _____ Mrs. Smith leaves the classroom.

Review

A. Match. Draw a line.

1. January, _____, March   a. dairy

2. This person answers phones in an office.   b. address

3. It is at the end of your arm.   c. aspirin

4. your home   d. bank

5. milk, cheese, butter   e. bread

6. not sunny   f. dime

7. medicine for a headache   g. doctor

8. a place for money   h. February

9. food for a sandwich   i. hand

10. ten cents   j. June

11. This person can work in a hospital.   k. cloudy

12. May, _____, July   l. receptionist

13. clothing for winter   m. ride

14. a place to buy food   n. shoes

15. You wear them on your feet.   o. supermarket

16. You _____ a bicycle.   p. sweater

B. Write three words for each unit.

Unit	Words	Unit	Words
Personal information	_____ _____ _____	Our Community	_____ _____ _____
Our Class	_____ _____ _____	Healthy Living	_____ _____ _____
Food	_____ _____ _____	Work	_____ _____ _____
Clothing	_____ _____ _____	Lifelong Learning and Review	_____ _____ _____

C. Find the page number from the Vocabulary List on pages 212 and 213 and write a sentence.

Phrase: marital status

Page number: _20_

Sentence: _He is single._

Phrase: extra large

Page number: _____

Sentence: _____

Phrase: go straight

Page number: _____

Sentence: _____

Word: checkup

Page number: _____

Sentence: _____

D. Find two new words from the Vocabulary List on pages 212 and 213.

Word: _____

Page number: _____

Sentence: _____

Word: _____

Page number: _____

Sentence: _____

E. Use the Grammar Reference on pages 214–216 and fill in the blanks.

1. a. I _____ married.

   b. We _____ students.

   c. You _____ hungry.

   d. They _____ thirsty.

   e. She _____ single.

2. a. I _____ milk.

   b. We _____ a bowl of soup.

   c. You _____ vegetables.

   d. They _____ tacos.

   e. She _____ a sandwich.

3. a. _____ your hands.

   b. _____ the phones.

   c. _____ meetings.

4. a. I can _____.

   b. Aki and Adriano can _____.

   c. We can't _____.

   d. The teacher can't _____.

F. Write the plural forms.

Singular	Plural
pear	
cookie	
banana	
egg	
tomato	

TEAM PROJECT ✓ Create a study guide

1. **COLLABORATE** Form a team with four or five students. In your team, you need:

Position	Job description	Student name
Student 1: Team Leader	Check that everyone speaks English. Check that everyone participates.	
Student 2: Writer	Organize and add sections to the study guide.	
Student 3: Artist	Decorate the study guide.	
Students 4/5: Spokespeople	Prepare a presentation.	

2. Complete your binder from this unit. Share the information from your binder with your group.

3. Use your binders to make a team binder. This will be a study guide for new students.

4. Decorate the study guide.

5. Present your study guide to the class.

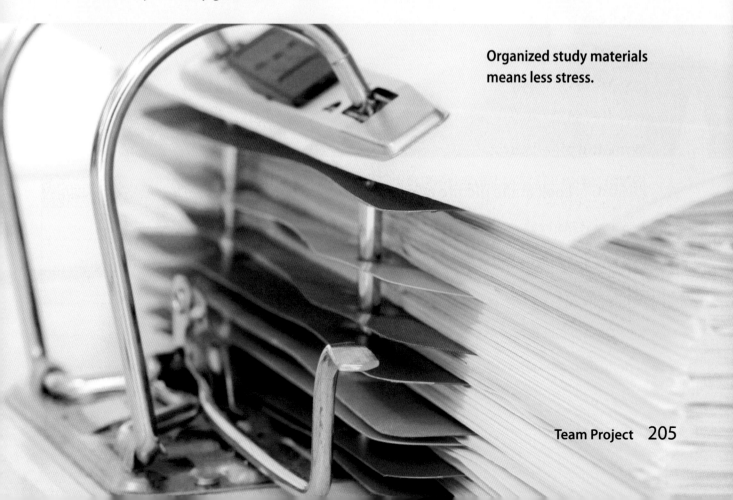

Organized study materials means less stress.

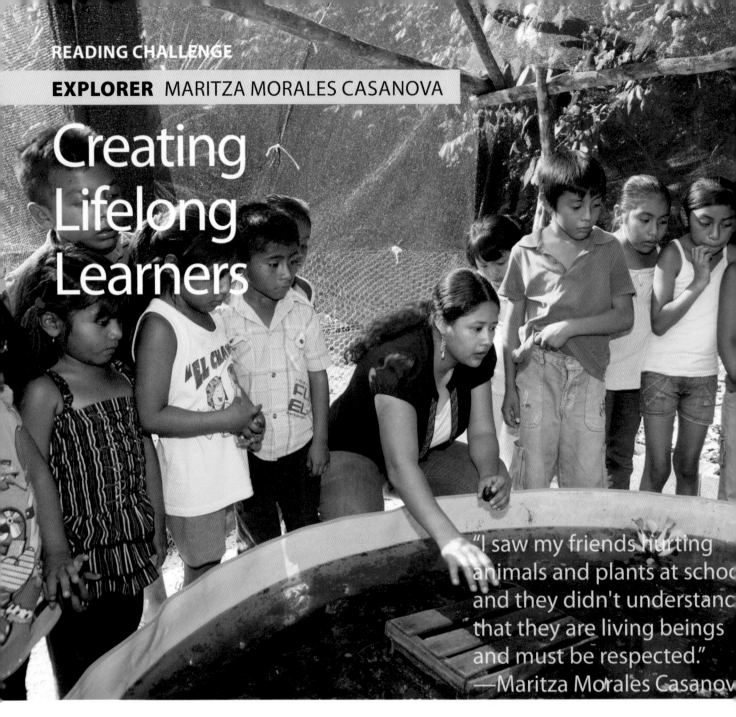

Creating Lifelong Learners

"I saw my friends hurting animals and plants at school and they didn't understand that they are living beings and must be respected."
—Maritza Morales Casanova

A. **PREDICT** Look at the picture and answer the questions.

1. Where is Maritza?

2. What is she doing?

B. **PREDICT** Look at the words. Draw lines to match the words and the definitions.

nature   the Earth

the planet   living things like plants and animals

lifelong learning   help someone or something be safe

take care   don't stop learning

C. **Read about Maritza Morales Casanova.**

> Maritza Morales Casanova is a teacher. She believes the nature around us is important. At the Ceiba Pentandra Park in Mexico, she and her fellow teachers show people how to take care of the planet. She wants everyone to learn and continue learning. She teaches her students to be lifelong learners. That's why most of the teachers at the park are children!

D. **Answer the questions about the paragraph.**

1. *What does Maritza do?*

   She's a _____.

2. *What* is the name of the park?

   _____.

3. *Where* is the park?

   _____.

4. *Who* are the teachers?

   _____.

E. **Practice asking and answering the questions in Exercise D.**

F. **SURVEY** **Ask five students about their favorite subjects. Complete the table. Write any new subjects in the spaces provided.**

A. What is your favorite subject?
B. My favorite subject is <u>science</u>.

Name	English	Math	Science	History	_____	_____
Maritza			✓			

People of the Reindeer

A Sami woman with a reindeer

Over the last four units, you have learned about different types of housing and transportation. You have also learned about different types of jobs. Now you will meet the Sami people from the Arctic region of Finland. The Sami people have a special type of housing and a very different type of transportation.

Before You Watch

A. Read the sentences. Match the word in bold to its meaning.

1. My **journey** was interesting because I visited many places in northern Europe.

2. We always sleep outside in a **tent** when we travel with our animals.

3. The **reindeer** usually eat the grass under the soft snow.

4. My people's **tradition** is to wear bright clothing with red and yellow colors.

a. something people do for a long time that never changes _____

b. a large animal with antlers that lives in cold places _____

c. a type of housing for outside used when you travel _____

d. traveling from one place to another _____

B. You are going to watch a video. Look at the pictures and read the captions. Match.

a. b. c.

1. These Sami people have traditional clothing. _____

2. On a journey, the Sami people live in tents. _____

3. The Sami people work with their reindeer. _____

C. Look at the pictures and read the captions in Exercise B again. What do you think the video is going to be about? Circle your choice.

a. The food the Sami people eat.

b. Winter snowstorms in northern Europe.

c. How the Sami people live and work.

d. The life of reindeer in the Arctic countries.

While You Watch

A. **Was your prediction correct? What is the video about? Complete the sentence in your own words.**

The video is about _____.

B. **Watch the video again. Circle the word you hear in each statement.**

1. The Sami people's reindeer move in (winter / spring).
2. The (farmers / children) travel with the reindeer, too.
3. This snow is hard. After (snowy / sunny) weather, it is soft.
4. (Soft / Hard) snow is good for the reindeer.
5. Well, that's all. It's time to (work / sleep).

C. **Put the events in order. Write the correct number on the line.**

_____ a. The Sami people move the reindeer together.

_____ b. A Sami man eats at the table in his home.

_____ c. A Sami man sits on the snow with his dog.

_____ d. A Sami baby in bright clothing plays outside.

_____ e. A Sami woman works outside her house.

_____ f. A Sami man sits next to a fire inside his tent.

After You Watch

A. **Describe the video. Complete each sentence with the correct verb.**

working	eating	burning	sitting	running

1. The Sami child is _____ berries.

2. The reindeer are _____ in the snow.

3. The Sami woman is _____ in the yard.

4. The fire is _____ inside the *goahti*.

5. The Sami man is _____ next to his dog.

B. What did you learn about the Sami people? Classify the words and phrases in the table. Check the correct category.

	Type of housing	Daily duty	Food
make a fire			
reindeer meat			
take care of children			
goahti			
berries			
move reindeer together			
pack tents			
flatbread			
watch the reindeer			

C. Look at the picture. Who do you know that uses a tent? Does the person live in the tent all the time? What is the tent used for?

EXAMPLE: We use a tent when we go camping and sleep in the woods. My family and I do not live in our tent. We live in a three-bedroom house.

D. Work in small groups. Describe a long journey that you made. Where did you go or come from? Share with the class.

EXAMPLE: My family and I traveled from Florida to New York. We drove in our car for 19 hours.

_____

_____

_____

STAND OUT BASIC VOCABULARY LIST

PRE-UNIT
Greetings
bye 3
goodbye 3
hello 3
hi 3
Study verbs
check 11
circle 7
listen 9
point 6
read 9
repeat 10
write 10

UNIT 1
Calendar
date 27
month 26
year 26
Months
April 26
August 26
December 26
February 26
January 26
July 26
June 26
March 26
May 26
November 26
October 26
September 26
Marital status
divorced 20
married 20
single 20
Personal information
address 23
application 31
birthplace 18
city 23
date of birth 27
from 17
live 19
name 14
state 23
zip code 23

UNIT 2
phone number 38
schedule 47
time 48
Classroom words
book 41
board 41
bookcase 41
computer 41
desk 41
file cabinet 41
CD 45
notebook 45
pen 45
pencil 45
plant 41
sit 46
stand 46
trash can 41
Location
behind 42
between 42
in 42
in the front 42
next to 42
on 42
Weather
cloudy 50
cold 50
foggy 50
hot 50
rainy 50
snowy 50
sunny 50
windy 50

UNIT 3
Dinner 65
hungry 65
thirsty 66
Food
apple 63
banana 63
bread 63
broccoli 71
butter 63
cake 74
candy 74

carrot 67
cheese 63
chicken 63
chips 67
chocolate 74
cookie 67
egg 63
fries 65
fruit 70
ground beef 68
ham 62
hamburger 65
ice cream 74
lettuce 63
mayonnaise 63
milk 63
onion 68
orange 63
pear 69
pepper 69
pie 74
potato 63
rice 65
salt 68
sandwich 62
spaghetti 68
taco 65
tomato 63
tuna fish 62
turkey 63
vegetables 65
water 63
yogurt 74
Measurements and containers
bag 69
can 69
jar 68
package 68
pound 68
Supermarket
dairy 71
fish 71
meat 71

UNIT 4
Clothing
blouse 87
coat 87

dress 87
pants 86
shirt 86
shoes 86
shorts 87
socks 87
sweater 87
Colors
black 93
brown 93
blue 93
gray 93
green 93
orange 93
pink 93
purple 93
red 93
white 93
yellow 93
Money
dime 95
dollar 95
nickel 95
penny 95
quarter 95
Shopping
cash register 95
extra large 93
large 93
medium 93
receipt 97
sale 98
size 93
small 93

UNIT 5
Directions
go straight 127
stop 127
turn left 127
turn right 127
Housing
apartment 117
condominium 118
house 117
mobile home 117
Places in the community
bank 126
bookstore 126

bus stop 115
clothing store 114
coffee shop 114
electronics store 114
fast food 115
hospital 126
hotel 115
pharmacy 114
post office 126
restaurant 115
shoe store 114
supermarket 114
Transportation
bicycle 120
bus 120
car 120
come 122
drive 121
get 122
go 122
ride 121
take 121
taxi 120
train 120
walk 121

UNIT 6
checkup 147
exercise 147
healthy 147
smoke 147
Ailments
backache 141
cold 141
cough 141
fever 141
headache 141
runny nose 141
sore throat 141
stomachache 141
Medicine
antacid 145
aspirin 145
cough syrup 145
Parts of Body
arm 139
back 139
ear 140
foot 139
hand 139
head 139

leg 139
mouth 140
neck 139
nose 139

UNIT 7
Evaluations
careful 172
cheerful 172
friendly 172
helpful 172
Occupations
administrative
assistant 168
bus driver 163
cashier 163
cook 164
custodian 165
doctor 163
employee 168
mail carrier 164
manager 164
nurse 164
receptionist 165
salesperson 163

student 163
teacher 163
worker 169
Work verbs
answer phones 168
make change 168
mop 168
schedule meetings 169
send memos 168
supervise employees 168
take breaks 169
talk to customers 168

UNIT 8
binder 186
divider 186
goal 195
highlighter pen 186
paper clip 186
sticky note 186

STAND OUT BASIC GRAMMAR REFERENCE

Simple Present

Subject	Verb	Example sentence
I, You, We, They	live take ride walk	I **live** in Mexico. You **take** the bus. We **ride** a bicycle. They **walk** to school.
He, She, It	live**s** take**s** ride**s** walk**s**	He **lives** in Irvine. He **takes** the bus. She **rides** a bicycle. She **walks** to work.

Simple Present

Subject	Verb	Example sentence
I, You, We, They	eat	I **eat** three meals a day.
He, She, It	sleeps	She **sleeps** seven hours a night.

Negative Simple Present

Subject	Verb		Example sentence
I, You, We, They	**don't**	eat	We **don't eat** three meals a day.
He, She, It	**doesn't**	sleep~~s~~	He **doesn't sleep** seven hours a night.

Simple Present: *Be*

Subject	*Be*	Example sentence
I	am	I **am** friendly.
He, She, It	is	She **is** friendly.
We, You, They	are	They **are** friendly.

Simple Present: *Be* (negative)

Subject	*Be* *(Negative)*	Example sentence
I	am not	I **am not** friendly.
He, She, It	is not	She **is not** friendly.
We, You, They	are not	They **are not** friendly.

Simple Present: *Have*

Subject	*Have*	Example sentence
I, You, We, They	have	I **have** two shirts.
He, She	has	She **has** a dress.

Possessive Adjectives

Subject	Possessive adjective	Example sentence
I	My	**My** phone number is 555-3456.
You	Your	**Your** address is 2359 Maple Drive.
He	His	**His** name is Edgar.
She	Her	**Her** name is Julie.
We	Our	**Our** last name is Perez.
They	Their	**Their** teacher is Mr. Jackson.

Prepositions of Location

a. It's **in the front of** the store.

b. It's **in the corner of** the store.

c. It's **in the middle of** the store.

d. It's **in the back of** the store.

e. It's **on the left side of** the store.

f. It's **on the right side of** the store.

How much and How many

Question		Answer
How much	(money) is the sweater?	It is $33.00.
How many	coats do you want?	I want three coats.

Yes/No Questions

Question	Answer
Do you buy clothing at a department store?	
Do you buy food at a supermarket?	Yes, I do.
Do you buy shoes at a shoe store?	No, I don't.

Imperatives

	Subject	Verb
Please	~~you~~	read
		open
		let me (look)
		sit down
		stand up

Present Continuous (right now)

Subject	*Be*	Base + *ing*	Example sentence
I	am	talking	I **am talking**.
He, She, It	is	sleeping	He **is sleeping**.
We, You, They	are	waiting	They **are waiting**.

Information Questions

Question word	Type of answer
What	information (receptionist)
Where	a place (Johnson Company)
When	a time or day (9–6) (Monday–Friday)
Who	a person (Martin)

Can

Subject	*Can*	Verb (base)	Example sentence
I, You, He, She, It, We, They	can	type	I can type.
		mop	He can mop floors.

Can't

Subject	*Can't*	Verb (base)	Example sentence
I, You, He, She, It, We, They	can't	type	I can't type.
		mop	He can't mop floors.

Affirmative Commands

	Verb		Example sentence
~~You~~	wash	your hands	Wash your hands.
	answer	the phones	Answer the phones.
	type	letters	Type the letters.

Negative Commands

	Verb			Example sentence
~~You~~	don't	wash	your hands	Don't wash your hands.
		answer	the phones	Don't answer the phones.
		type	letters	Don't type the letters.

PHOTO CREDITS

01 **(tl)** Portra Images/Getty Images, **(tc)** Portra Images/Getty Images, **(tr)** Mark Edward Atkinson/ Tracey Lee/Getty Images, **(bl)** Hero Images/Getty Images, **(bc)** Jade/Getty Images, **(br)** Seth Joel/ Getty Images; 02 **(b)** Erica Shires/Crave/Corbis; 06 **(tl)** Andrey Orletsky/Shutterstock.com, **(tr)** Blvdone/Shutterstock.com; 07 **(tl)** Photos.com, **(tc)** IndexOpen, **(tc)** Photos.com, **(tr)** Photos. com; 09 **(bl)** arisara/Shutterstock.com, **(bc)** Africa Studio/Shutterstock.com, **(br)** Champion Studio/ Shutterstock.com; 10 **(tc)** Champion Studio/ Shutterstock.com, **(tc)** OliverSved/Shutterstock.com, **(cl)** arisara/Shutterstock.com, **(c)** BeautyBlowFlow/ Shutterstock.com, **(cr)** Africa Studio/Shutterstock. com, **(br)** Champion Studio/Shutterstock.com; 12–13 YOAN VALAT/Corbis Wire/Corbis; 14 Inspiron.Dell. Vector/Shutterstock.com; 20 **(tl)** Oliver Eltinger/ Fancy/Corbis, **(cr)** Fiona Conrad/Crave/Corbis, **(bl)** VStock/Alamy; 21 **(cl)** Photos.com, **(c)** ImageSource/ SuperStock, **(cr)** BananaStock/Alamy; 23 **(t)** Fotoluminate LLC/Shutterstock.com, **(b)** Vacclav/ Shutterstock.com; 24 **(t)** Beboy/Shutterstock.com, **(c)** Mark Segal/Index Stock Imagery/Getty Images, **(b)** Bob Mahoney/The Image Works; 27 GORDON WILTSIE/National Geographic Creative; 28 artcphotos/ Shutterstock.com; 29 ©Cengage Learning; 30 A and N Photography/Shutterstock.com; 31 **(bl)** VStock / Alamy, **(bc)** Fiona Conrad/Crave/Corbis, **(br)** Oliver Eltinger/Fancy/Corbis; 32 **(tl)** michaeljung/ Shutterstock.com, **(tr)** Diego Cervo/Shutterstock. com, **(cl)** Dmitry Kalinovsky/Shutterstock.com, **(cr)** eurobanks/Shutterstock.com; 34 **(tl)** MIKEY SCHAEFER/National Geographic Creative, **(tr)** Courtesy of Sarah Marquis, **(cl)** Rolando Pujol/EPA/ Newscom, **(cr)** Rolex Awards/François Schaer; 36–37 ED KASHI/National Geographic Creative; 45 **(tl)** optimarc/Shutterstock.com, **(tc)** Vladislav Lyutov/ Shutterstock.com, **(tr)** Africa Studio/Shutterstock. com, **(cl)** naipung/Shutterstock.com, **(c)**

Early Spring/Shutterstock.com, **(cr)** Jason / Alamy, **(bl)** Wavebreakmedia/Shutterstock.com, **(bc)** Rangizzz/Shutterstock.com, **(br)** Christian Delbert/Shutterstock.com; 48 Jarrod Ligrani/ Shutterstock.com; 50 **(tl)** Manamana/Shutterstock. com, **(tr)** Meunierd/Shutterstock.com, **(cr)** Nadezda Stoyanova/Shutterstock.com, **(bl)** john norman / Alamy, **(bc)** ivylingpy/Shutterstock. com, **(br)** Tupungato/Shutterstock.com; 52 **(tl)** sirirak kaewgorn/Shutterstock.com, **(tc)** S_Photo/ Shutterstock.com, **(tc)** Peshkova/Shutterstock.com, **(tr)** fototi photography/Shutterstock.com;

53 ©Cengage Learning; 56 **(tl)** Photos.com, **(cl)** Photos.com, **(cl)** Rido/Shutterstock.com, **(bl)** Photos.com; 57 Anibal Trejo/Shutterstock.com; 58 National Geographic Creative; 60-61 GERD LUDWIG/National Geographic Creative; 65 **(bl)** J Shepherd/Ocean/Corbis, **(bc)** NatashaPhoto/ Shutterstock.com, **(bc)** Foodio/Shutterstock.com, **(br)** Ildi Papp/Shutterstock.com

67 **(tl)** Tei Sinthipsomboon/Shutterstock.com, **(tc)** Ozgur Coskun/Shutterstock.com, **(tc)** Kati Molin/Shutterstock.com, **(tr)** Christian Draghici/ Shutterstock.com, **(cl)** Ramon Antinolo/Shutterstock. com, **(c)** Valentyn Volkov/Shutterstock.com, **(cr)** science photo/Shutterstock.com

68 **(tl)** Nitr/Shutterstock.com; 69 **(tl)** Guzel Studio/ Shutterstock.com, **(cl)** Guzel Studio/Shutterstock. com, **(c)** Guzel Studio/Shutterstock.com, **(tr)** Pack/ Shutterstock.com **(c)** Pack/Shutterstock.com, **(cr)**

Pack/Shutterstock.com; 70 **(tl)** Ramon Antinolo/ Shutterstock.com, **(tr)** Ramon Antinolo/Shutterstock. com, **(tl)** Kati Molin/Shutterstock.com **(tr)** Tei Sinthipsomboon/Shutterstock.com, **(cl)** Candus Camera/Shutterstock.com, **(cr)** Ozgur Coskun/ Shutterstock.com, **(cl)** K2 PhotoStudio/Shutterstock. com, **(cr)** Mmkarabella/Shutterstock.com, **(1)** Photos. com, **(2)** Photos.com, **(3)** Photos.com, **(4)** IndexOpen; 72 **(tr)** Nick Rains/Terra/Corbis; 74 **(tl)** Africa Studio/ Shutterstock.com, **(tc)** Brent Hofacker/Shutterstock. com, **(tc)** Dusan Zidar/Shutterstock.com, **(tr)** Amarita/Shutterstock.com, **(tr)** HandmadePictures/ Shutterstock.com, **(c)** Brent Hofacker/Shutterstock. com, **(cr)** Africa Studio/Shutterstock.com; 75 **(bl)** Rhienna Cutler/Getty Images, **(bc)** Ronnie Kaufman/ Getty Images, **(br)** glyn/Shutterstock.com; 77 © Cengage Learning, 78 **(tl)** Candus Camera/ Shutterstock.com, **(tc)** Brent Hofacker/Shutterstock. com, **(tr)** Amarita/Shutterstock.com

(cl) Christian Draghici/Shutterstock.com, **(c)** Brent Hofacker/Shutterstock.com, **(c)** Mmkarabella/ Shutterstock.com; 81 **(b)** kongsak sumano/ Shutterstock.com; 82 **(t)** ©Catherine Jaffee/National Geographic Creative; **(br)** Shaiith/Shutterstock. com; 84–85 The Licensing Project/Offset; 87 **(cl)** Photos.com, **(C)** Photos.com, **(cl)** IndexOpen, **(c)** Jack Hollingsworth/Blend Images/Getty Images, **(cr)** Thomas Northcut/Photodisc/Getty Images, **(bl)** D. Hurst/Alamy, **(bc)** Photos.com, **(br)** Clipart; 91 Fiphoto/Shutterstock.com; 93 Radius/Corbis; 95 **(tl)** RTimages/Shutterstock.com, **(tc)** RTimages/ Shutterstock.com, **(tr)** RTimages/Shutterstock.com, **(cl)** United States Government/Public Domain, **(c)** United States Government/Public Domain, **(cr)** United States Government/Public Domain, **(c)** United States Government/Public Domain, **(cr)** United States Government/Public Domain, **(cr)** United States Government/Public Domain, **(cr)** United States Government/Public Domain, **(cr)** United States Government/Public Domain, **(c)** United States Government/Public Domain, **(bl)** United States Government/Public Domain, **(bc)** United States Government/Public Domain, **(bc)** United States Government/Public Domain, **(bc)** United States Government/Public Domain, **(bc)** United States Government/Public Domain, **(br)** United States Government/Public Domain; 96 **(tr)** United States Government/Public Domain, **(tr)** United States Government/Public Domain, **(tr)** United States Government/Public Domain, **(tr)** United States Government/Public Domain, **(tr)** United States Government/Public Domain, **(cr)** United States Government/Public Domain, **(cr)** United States Government/Public Domain, **(cr)** United States Government/Public Domain, **(cr)** United States Government/Public Domain, **(br)** United States Government/Public Domain, **(br)** United States Government/Public Domain; 97 **(tl)** Photos.com, **(tr)** Photos.com, **(cl)** Photos.com, **(cr)** IndexOpen, **(bl)** Photos.com, **(br)** Jack Hollingsworth/Blend Images/ Getty Images; 98 Oscar Hernandez; 101 ©Cengage Learning; 102 **(1)** Photos.com, **(2)** Photos.com, **(3)** Thomas Northcut/Photodisc/Getty Images, **(4)** Photos.com, **(5)** Photos.com, **(6)** IndexOpen, **(7)** Jack Hollingsworth/Blend Images/Getty Images, **(8)** D. Hurst/Alamy; 103 **(b)** Jorge Salcedo/ Shutterstock.com; 105 Africa Studio/Shutterstock. com; 106 Courtesy of Sarah Marquis; 107 Chrupka/ Shutterstock.com; 108 Pedrosala/Shutterstock.com; 111 Mark Leong/Redux; 113–114 © Liesl Marelli;

114 **(1)** fiphoto/Shutterstock.com, **(2)** Niki Love/ Shutterstock.com, **(3)** fiphoto/Shutterstock.com, **(4)** Dotshock/Shutterstock.com, **(5)** Mangostock/ Shutterstock.com, **(6)** Panna Studio/Shutterstock.com; 118 **(tl)** Rodenberg Photography/Shutterstock.com, **(tc)** Tim Collins/Shutterstock.com, **(tr)** Rudy Umans/ Shutterstock.com; 119 **(tl)** Kevin Peterson/Photodisc/ Getty Images, **(tc)** Hemera Photodisc, **(tr)** Hemera Photodisc; 120 **(tl)** zentilia/Shutterstock.com, **(tl)** Art Konovalov/Shutterstock.com, **(cl)** guroldinneden/ Shutterstock.com, **(tc)** luckyraccoon/Shutterstock.com

(c) after6pm/Shutterstock.com; 123 **(tl)** kristian sekulic/Getty Images, **(tc)** Maridav/Shutterstock. com, **(tr)** lightpoet/Shutterstock.com; 129 ©Cengage Learning; 131 **(tl)** lzf/Shutterstock.com, **(tr)** blvdone/ Shutterstock.com; 133 Radius Images/Alamy; 134 Mikey Schaefer/National Geographic Creative; 136–137 Corneliu Cazacu; 139 BROOKE WHATNALL/ National Geographic Creative; 141 **(tl)** Gpointstudio/ Shutterstock.com, **(tc)** wavebreakmedia/Shutterstock. com, **(tr)** Maskot/Getty Images, **(cl)** Alexander Raths/ Shutterstock.com, **(c)** Stefano Cavoretto/Shutterstock. com, **(cr)** Photographee.eu/Shutterstock.com; 142 **(b)** lofoto/Shutterstock.com; 149 **(tl)** Mark Anderson/Rubberball/Alamy, **(tc)** Amy Eckert/ UpperCut Images/Getty Images, **(tr)** EDHAR/ Shutterstock.com; 153 © Cengage Learning; 154 ALEX TREADWAY/National Geographic Creative; 158 Ernesto Mastrascusa/EPA/Newscom; 160–161 Abner Kingman / Aurora Photos; 165 **(tl)** Helen King/Comet/Corbis, **(cl)** Ian Lishman/Juice/Corbis, **(bl)** Oskari Porkka/Shutterstock.com; 167 auremar/ Shutterstock.com;

168 **(1)** Helen King/Comet/Corbis, **(2)** StockLite/ Shutterstock.com, **(3)** Hiya Images/Fancy/Corbis, **(4)**

Oskari Porkka/Shutterstock.com; 169 **(tl)** Racorn/ Shutterstock.com, **(tr)** Tim Pannell/Crave/Corbis; 171 kzenon/iStock/Getty Images Plus/Getty Images; 172 Dmitry Kalinovsky/Shutterstock.com; 173 Eliza Snow/E+/Getty Images; 174 **(tl)** Piyato/Shutterstock. com, **(tc)** Walther S/Shutterstock.com, **(tr)** Arcady/ Shutterstock.com; 176 **(tl)** Elena Elisseeva/ Shutterstock.com; 177 **(tr)** ©Cengage Learning

178 **(1)** Andrey_Popov/Shutterstock.com, **(2)** light poet/Shutterstock.com, **(3)** racorn/Shutterstock. com, **(4)** Karramba Production/Shutterstock. com, **(5)** Dmitry Kalinovsky/Shutterstock.com, **(6)** Cultura/Zero Creatives/Getty Images, **(7)** Pressmaster/Shutterstock.com, **(8)** wavebreakmedia/ Shutterstock.com; 179 **(1)** Oskari Porkka/ Shutterstock.com, **(2)** StockLite/Shutterstock.com, **(3)** Hiya Images/Fancy/Corbis, **(4)** michaeljung/ Shutterstock.com; 180 **(1)** Piyato/Shutterstock. com, **(2)** Arcady/Shutterstock.com, **(3)** Walther S/ Shutterstock.com; 181 **(b)** Catherine Karnow/ Encyclopedia/Corbis; 182 Rick Stanley/National Geographic Creative; 184–185 PAUL NICKLEN/ National Geographic Creative; 186 **(tl)** kyoshino/ Getty Images, **(cl)** Feng Yu/Shutterstock.com, **(bl)** Warwick Lister-Kaye/Getty Images, **(tr)** leungchopan/ Shutterstock.com, **(cr)** kai keisuke/Shutterstock. com, **(br)** robophobic/Shutterstock.com; 192 By Ian Miles-Flashpoint Pictures/Alamy; 195 hiroshitoyoda/ Shutterstock.com; 198 AbleStock/Index Stock Imagery/Photolibrary; 201 ©Cengage Learning; 205 rtbilder/Shutterstock.com; 206 Rolex Awards/ François Schaer; 208 PhotoDisc/Getty Images; 209 **(cl)** ©Cengage Learning **(c)** ©Cengage Learning, **(cr)** ©Cengage Learning; 211 ©Cengage Learning;

STAND OUT BASIC SKILLS INDEX

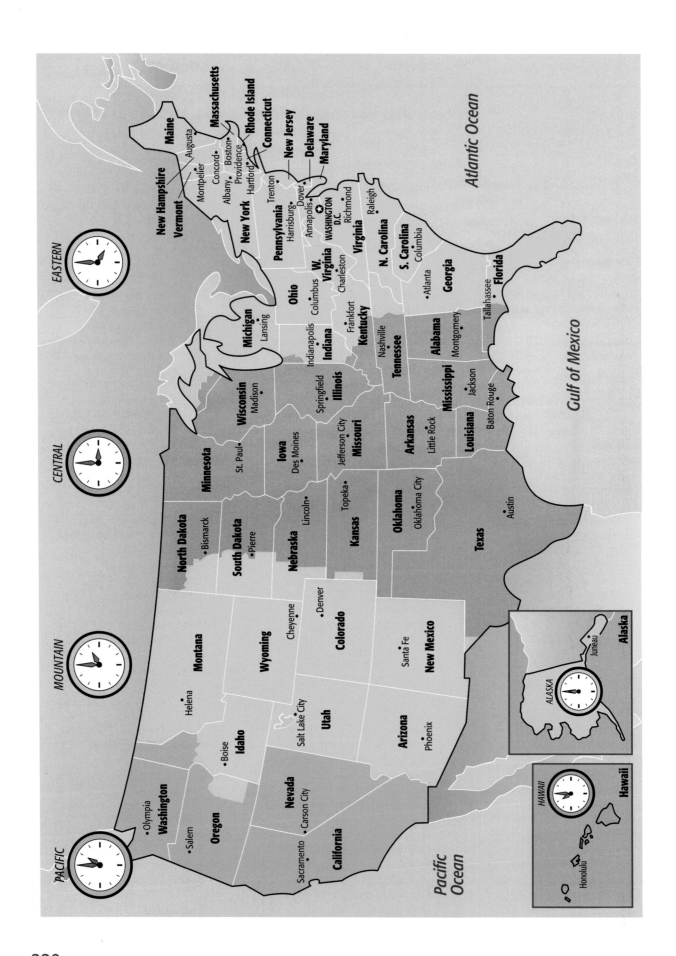